LOVING IN HIS WAY

HIS TENDER MERCIES: BOOK 2

T.K. CHAPIN

Branch Publishing

Version: 12.15.2019

ISBN: 1675789622

ISBN-13: 978-1675789629

My Prayer Journal

Be sure to check out the companion prayer book on Amazon.com. Order your copy today and start your journey toward a more rich and vibrant prayer life with the Lord.

View on Amazon

Dedicated to my loving wife.
For all the years she has put up with me
And many more to come.

CONTENTS

CHAPTER 1

*P*raying her sister would make it over to her house safely, Courtney McAdams questioned God's timing on her sister's reappearance in her life. She had just finished her schooling to become a dental hygienist four months ago and started a job at *Spokane Smiles* last week. Having her sister reemerge only meant one thing to Courtney—drama. Her sister, Taylor, had two children and one on the way. Her little two-bedroom apartment would soon go from a quiet and tranquil refuge from the world to a place that was loud, chaotic, and full of uncertainty.

A knock soon sounded at the front door, and Courtney rose from the couch. Breathing a deep sigh as she walked, she prayed for strength for the coming moments and days ahead. *Help me, Lord,* she prayed as her hand turned the doorknob and opened it.

Seeing her sister face-to-face moved Courtney with compassion. Taylor's blonde hair was disheveled, and a fresh open cut rested on her left cheek. Tears moistened her cheeks and mixed with mascara from her eyelashes. Her two boys were wrapped around each of her legs, Todd, age two, and Blaze, just barely one year old. With a diaper bag around her shoulder and a car seat in each hand, her sister looked like she had barely escaped Drake's rampage with her life.

Courtney's heart dipped into her stomach as guilt washed over her. She had only been thinking of herself, of her own discomfort in having her sister stay.

Taking a step toward her sister, Courtney crashed the threshold of the doorway and took hold of the car seats. She set them aside and then wrapped her arms around her sister and held her for a long moment. If only that hug could give her sister the love Courtney knew she needed.

"Thank you so much, Courtney."

"It's what family is for, right?" Pulling back from her sister, she wiped a tear from her cheek and then they all came into the apartment. Courtney shut the door. Going into the kitchen to heat water in the kettle for tea, she could hear her sister sniffling as she sat down in the living room. Turning her head, she saw Todd and Blaze stroking their mother's hair and trying to comfort her. A wave of uneasiness rose up within her. It didn't seem right that these little boys were in charge of helping their mother feel better. Exiting the kitchen quickly, she came over into the living room and to the two boys. She grabbed her nephews' hands and guided the two of them down the hallway to the spare bedroom the three of them would be staying in. She hadn't seen them in months, and although they didn't seem to remember her, they weren't afraid of her either.

She searched the room far and wide for something to keep the two boys occupied, but she didn't have much in the way of entertainment for children. Finally finding some copy paper and pens, she set the two of them down on the floor and returned to the living room and kitchen.

Taylor wasn't on the couch.

Suddenly, a scream sounded from the bathroom. Courtney's heart soared as she turned and ran down to the door in the hall. Trying the handle, she found it locked.

She knocked. "What's going on, Tay? You okay?"

"There's blood! Lots of it."

Courtney's pulse skyrocketed. "What? What do you mean? Let me in!"

She stammered as she tried to speak through the crying. "He hit me in the stomach, Courtney."

Trying the handle again, she started pounding. "Open the door, Taylor! Open the door!"

A moment passed and the door opened. Her sister's face was downcast. Touching her belly, which wasn't even a bump yet, she shook her head as her words tumbled out of her mouth, dripping with sorrow. "I don't think my little bean is going to make it. It was dark blood."

"We'll get you to the hospital right now. Let's go." Grabbing her hand, Courtney started down the hall. "You head to the car. I'll grab the boys."

Courtney hurried down the hallway to the spare bedroom and opened the door. Blaze and Todd had been occupied by the paper and pens, but they had favored the pens. The two young boys had written all over the walls, bedsheets, and desk in a matter of minutes.

"Wow. The two of you really went all out in here. Silly boys."

Scooping them up into her arms, she hurried out the bedroom and down the hall. Stopping in the living room, she grabbed the diaper bag and car seats and headed out to the car.

At the hospital they did blood work and an ultrasound and determined that the baby had indeed been lost. When the doctor broke the news to Taylor, she became distraught and so overwhelmed that she started groaning. Courtney took the boys down to the hospital cafeteria to get a bite to eat and let their mother digest the news.

Sitting in a booth with the boys as they ate their Pop Tarts, Courtney felt for the first time that evening that she could peel away and call her mother, Rhonda, who lived eight hours away in Blackfoot, Idaho. Staying within a few feet of the booth, she bit on a nail as she waited for her mother to answer.

"Hello?"

"Hey, Mom."

"Courtney? Why are you calling so late? It's ten o'clock at night."

"I'm at the hospital . . . with Taylor."

"Oh, no. What happened? What'd he do this time?"

Courtney's throat clenched. She knew the words she had to say wouldn't come easily or be enjoyable to her mother. She dug deep within her reservoirs for courage but came up empty.

"Hello? Courtney? Are you there?"

"Yes, I'm here." Wiping her eyes of stray tears, she shook her head. *Lord, strengthen me . . .*

"What happened? Did he hit her again? Some father he'll be to that new baby!"

"She lost the baby, Mom."

The airwaves went silent between them.

Just then, a Pop Tart hit the floor of the cafeteria, sliding as it landed near a rack of potato chips. Glancing over, she saw Blaze jumping up and down on the booth excitedly as Todd giggled hysterically. Courtney's mind flashed back to the living room in her apartment and seeing those two boys comforting their mother. The pained faces on the young children's faces as they tried to mend their broken mother back together. That wasn't their job. Their job was to be children, to have fun. Suddenly, she got a sick feeling in her stomach.

"I'm sorry, Mom, but I have to go."

A long-winded sigh sounded from the other end of the call and then her mother's tone sharpened. "Is Taylor done with that buffoon yet? Or is killing their child okay with her too?"

"I'm sure she's done with him, Mom. Pray for her. I'll keep you updated."

Getting back up to the hospital room a short while later, her heart and steps stopped short when she saw Drake standing by her sister's bedside. He was holding her hand.

"Daddy!" the boys shouted in unison as they went into the room toward Taylor's abuser and not their biological father.

"Hey, my dudes!" As Courtney saw Drake drop to his knees and embrace the two boys, her insides somersaulted as her anger waxed hot and that feeling in her stomach grew in size.

Trying to keep things civil, Courtney smiled politely at him and asked for a moment alone with her sister. Drake willingly went out into the hallway with the boys. Coming closer to her sister's hospital bedside, she began to cry and shake her head.

"Why's he here, Taylor?"

"I called him. He lost his child too."

"Are you kidding me right now?" Courtney shook her head as she took a step back and pointed to the door. "It's *his* fault! You could've died too!"

"You're being dramatic. I was being really mean to him. You don't understand at all." Taylor looked past Courtney toward the door. "He's the father those boys never had."

"Because he's not their dad!" Shaking her head, Courtney tried to reason with her. "Please don't do this, Taylor. You can't trust a man who abuses you."

"He said he was sorry. It won't happen again. It's not like it goes on all the time or anything. You're being dramatic."

"But I don't—"

"Enough!"

The shout rippled through Courtney's chest, cutting to the core of her heart.

"It's not like you really wanted us all staying in your apartment, anyway."

"You're right! But you're family and we watch out for each other, and I'm telling you that Drake isn't done."

"I don't want to hear it anymore! I'm sick of it!"

"He hit you less than a few hours ago! And killed your baby!"

"Get out!"

"What?"

"I said get out of here. Leave me alone."

"Fine." Grabbing her purse, Courtney dried her cheeks and exited the hospital room. Walking over to the boys, she got down to their eye level and hugged them tightly as she prayed over them. *Lord, protect them. Protect these innocent little lives, Jesus. Somehow, deliver them out of this.* Then, she did the impossible. Peering into their innocent eyes, she smiled. "I love you, boys. I'll see you around. Okay?"

"Love you!" they both said to her.

Standing upright, she couldn't even look at Drake. She started down the hall toward the exit, but Drake called out to her. "I need the car seats."

"I'll bring them in."

On the drive back to her apartment a short while later, she thought about calling her mother but decided to let her sleep, at least for tonight. Arriving home, she walked into her apartment and the silence was a painful reminder. A reminder that she wasn't interested in her sister staying just a few short hours ago and now, she'd give anything to keep her sister and those boys protected there with her. Grabbing a bottle of cleaner and a washcloth, since sleep was the last thing on her mind, she went into the spare room and started cleaning the artwork Todd and Blaze had left all over the room. After she finished the walls, she stripped the bed of the sheets and threw them into the wash, then began on the desk. As she finished, she had a layer of sweat on her forehead. Wiping the sweat with her forearm, she sat down in the office chair.

She was reminded of how her husband, Drew, had used that same desk for years. She recalled when they first got it when they lived in their house out in Nine Mile Falls, a small community outside of Spokane. Since the day they got the desk until the day he died, he'd sit for hours in his study, writing sermons and stories and reading his Bible.

Opening the lower right drawer, she saw a stack of his journals. He would write prayers and conversations he'd had with God in them. In the two years since his passing, Courtney hadn't been able to read much of them. Each time she'd start, her heart would crumble into a million pieces and she'd break down.

Retrieving one from the drawer, she opened it up and began to read.

6/8/2010

Bible reading: Genesis 13-18

Focus: Abraham had a lot of waiting to do when it came to the Lord's will being accomplished through his son Isaac's birth. He had to trust God, and Abraham's belief was credited to him as righteousness. Not his doings or conduct, which weren't perfect by any means, but his faith was the key component to pleasing God.

Prayers:

My first prayer of today is for my wife, Courtney. We received the news yesterday that I am unable to have children, and I know it pains her more than it pains me. Though I am glad it is me and not her, I can't help but worry about her heart, Lord. We had dreamed of one day having children, and I know she has dreamed of having a family since she was a little girl. In this way, my heart continually drifts to worry for her, yet I know in my soul that You are in full control of my life, of our life. Help this disbelief that is lodged in me and in Your servant's heart. Help me become more surrendered to You not only in this way, but in all ways, Lord. I pray for my wife that she is comforted in her heartache. Only You can wipe away those tears in her soul. Strengthen her heart, Lord, and help me to love her more like You love the church.

Stopping as it was too hard to continue, Courtney peered up at the ceiling and shook her head as tears streamed down her cheeks. "Why'd You have to take him from me, Lord? What was the purpose?"

Instantly, she was reminded of her late husband's words at his own father's funeral years ago. "Nobody is ours, but on loan from God."

She thought of her sister and those two precious little boys and then prayed again. "I need Your strength, Lord. My heart gravitates toward worry when it comes to my sister and those two innocent children. What I saw in such a short time tonight was heartbreaking and disturbing. Let my heart lean on You. Help me to trust in You. Protect those three, Lord. Protect them."

Replacing the journal in the drawer of the desk, she shut it and left the room.

Courtney didn't hear from Taylor for four months afterward, and her sister hadn't returned her calls during that time either. Then late one night in October, pounding on her front door sounded in the middle of the night.

She awoke in a panic-stricken state and glanced at the alarm clock on her nightstand. It was just after midnight. Slipping her robe on, Courtney went out and answered the door.

Her sister was crying but not wounded this time.

"I'm homeless, Courtney." Setting her hands on the top of her two sons' heads, she peered into Courtney's eyes. "We're homeless."

"Come in."

Courtney had to work the next day, so right after getting them situated in the spare bedroom, she went back to bed.

The next morning, after she was done getting ready for work, she was pouring a cup of coffee quietly as her sister slept on the couch. Hearing her sister's phone suddenly buzz on the coffee table, she walked into the living room and glanced at the screen. It was a notification from an app. She was about to turn and leave when she caught sight of a needle next to the phone on the coffee table. Her heart dipped as she recalled Taylor's checkered past and her bout of drug use after losing their father, Frank, four years ago.

Peering down the hallway toward the spare bedroom where the boys were sleeping, she hesitated to deal with it in the moment. If she forced her sister out right then, the boys would be homeless too.

She left the apartment and walked out to the parking lot.

As she walked toward her car, her mind bombarded her with thoughts. *What if the kids wake up? They could get the needle and hurt themselves. You have drugs in your home! You have to get to work, and you can't take another sick day after that week you missed a month ago for strep throat.*

Then her mind went quiet and one thought came into her consciousness. *What would Drew do?* Knowing he would turn to the Bible, she thought of Proverbs 3:27. *Do not withhold good from those to whom it is due, when it is in your power to act.*

9

She slammed the car keys into her purse and headed back to the apartment. Peering up at the sky, she shrugged. "I don't know how this is all going to work out, but I'm going to trust You, God. Trust that everything is somehow going to work out."

Going back into the apartment, she shut the door quietly behind her and dropped her purse beside the couch. Taking a knee on the carpet near her sister's face on the couch, Courtney gently shrugged her awake.

"What do you want? I'm so tired."

"There's a needle on my coffee table."

Taylor jerked her body upright and plucked the needle from the table. Rising to her feet, she hurried over into the kitchen and threw it away.

"Sorry, I'm on insulin . . ."

Courtney stood up and went into the kitchen. Her eyes tried to capture her sister's attention. *"Taylor."*

"What? You have a problem with insulin users?"

Rushing to her, Courtney grabbed her left arm and shot the sleeve up. Track marks littered her arm. "Insulin?"

Forcefully pulling her arm away from her, Taylor scowled. "Don't judge me."

"You need help, Sis. It's okay to need help!"

"No!" She pointed to the hallway, trying not to get too loud. "I will lose my boys if I get help! It was different after Dad died. I didn't have kids to take care of and I could just focus on getting sober. I have children now. How am I going to take care of them and me? I just found out their father passed away in prison. I am alone with this!"

Courtney stayed quiet, thankful that her sister had at least thought about it. Taylor went over to the couch and sat down. She began to cry and then she folded her face into her hands.

Joining her on the couch, Courtney turned toward her.

"Maybe you can do one of those outpatient treatments and still take care of the kids?"

"I don't think that will work for me. There is this one place, *Flowing Meadows* out in Wyoming. They said they could take me on a sponsorship, paid in full because I have children. It's for three months, but the boys can't go."

"Maybe Mom can take them?"

Taylor began to cry into her hands again. "I know Mom won't do it. They're too much trouble for her in her old age."

Scooting closer to her on the couch, she smoothed a hand over Taylor's back. "Then I'll do it."

Lifting her moistened eyes, she shook her head. "But how? You have a job and everything."

"I don't know how it'll work, but we have to make it work."

———

POUNDING AWAY ON THE KEYBOARD at five o'clock in the morning one November morning, Brian Dunlap smoothed a hand over his face as he saw the time in the lower right corner of his computer screen. *Only two more hours and then I have to get dressed,* he reminded himself. He had been waking up at four every morning for the last five days in a row in the hopes of getting ahead with work. He had to balance replying to client emails, fixing random issues on the website, and completing the ad copy for the series of new advertising he was hoping to roll out for next week's Black Friday sale he was having for puppychowdirect.com, his online e-commerce site. His eleven-year-old daughter, Lucy, was arriving that morning to spend her one weekend a month with him. He knew he'd be buried in work no matter what come Monday morning, but at least these last five days of effort would make it less painful.

Suddenly, it was seven o'clock. His insides cleaved as he still had five more ads to design. *At least the ad copy is done.*

Rising up from his computer chair, he passed by his workout room that was covered in dust and headed for the shower. Inside the en-suite bathroom, he kicked dirty towels out of the way and started his shower.

As he let the hot, steaming water crash over his body, he reached over and pressed the button that fired up the massage jets. Then he remembered a different task on his to-do list that was even more important than the ad copy. He had forgotten to update the new design for the banner at the top of the website.

He shut off the shower and quickly grabbed his robe and headed back to the office. His hair still wet, and nothing but a robe on, he opened up his website's back end system and started uploading the new design banner. After uploading it, he saw an issue and had to make an adjustment before re-uploading. Finally done, he stood up to leave his office when his doorbell chimes sang through the house.

Peering at the clock, he saw it was 7:30 AM. His ex-wife, Melissa, and his daughter, Lucy, had arrived.

Shuffling quickly out of his office, he tightened his robe and slicked his hair back on his way to answer the door. Stopping in the foyer, he grabbed the random moving box that was sitting against the wall and moved it into the coat closet to hide the fact that he still hadn't finished unpacking in the two months he had lived there. Peering through the foyer toward the living room, he thought about how he had forgotten to clean up the night before. Breathing deeply, he turned toward the door and opened it with a smile on his face.

"Ladies."

"Hi, Daddy!" Lucy moved closer to him and wrapped her arms around him. She might've been growing up and starting to become interested in boys, but she was still his little girl at heart. Warmly embracing her, he smiled and kissed the top of her head.

"I've missed you, Princess."

"I missed you too." Lucy walked in past him while he was left alone at the door with Melissa. As soon as Lucy was out of earshot, Melissa started in on him.

"What's the deal with the bathrobe? You knew we were coming, right? Or did you forget?"

"I didn't forget. I was finishing up some work stuff." She was about to say something more, but he held up a hand. "I have to go. My daughter is here."

Brian shut the door and then went into the kitchen. The sink was full of dishes and empty pizza boxes, and takeout containers filled the kitchen island and counters. He started to clean up and then moved on to the rest of the house. It took him almost two hours to clean, and it irritated him that it cut into a portion of his time with his daughter. That evening, as he pillowed his head, he returned to his thoughts last month about hiring someone to take care of the mundane minutiae of life. He had tried several times with a local hiring agency in the past, but each person they sent ended up needing more direction than he could give them. He needed someone who would handle things without having their hand held every moment. *How do I find someone like that, Lord?* he asked God as he prayed about the situation that evening.

The following morning, Brian and Lucy got dressed and went to church. After going to the first service, he and Lucy both served in the toddlers' class during the second service. Brian served in the class every Sunday, but Lucy only did on the one weekend a month she was with him. Lucy didn't attend church at her mother's house much, to his dismay, but Melissa wouldn't budge on it whenever he brought it up.

After prayer and story time in the Sunday school class, it was time for snacks. Lucy began setting out napkins, and Brian followed behind her pouring out cereal for each child. As he poured a handful onto a napkin, a frantic woman appeared in the doorway of the classroom.

"Hey. Am I too late?"

Lifting his gaze, Brian looked over at the doorway. There was a beautiful woman standing there, a child on each hip and a look of desperation in her eyes. Her eyes were red and swollen, and it appeared to him that she might've been crying or not sleeping, possibly both. Moved with compassion for the stranger, Brian handed his daughter the container of cereal in his hand and approached the woman in the doorway.

He smiled. "It's never too late."

She laughed lightly, but he could tell it was fake and forced. The woman gently placed the two little boys over the child gate. "Thank goodness! I needed a break."

"What?" Taken aback by the mother's comment, he felt a measure of repulsion flinch inside him. "You will be in the sanctuary, right? You're not, like, leaving?"

"No, I'm not leaving. I'll be in the sanctuary! I'm so sorry, it's just been hard. They are my nephews and they're just staying with me while their mother . . . gets well. My church didn't have a children's class during service, and they cannot handle being in service with me, so here we are!"

His heart eased and shifted again to compassion. Turning his gaze toward the boys, he watched them as they sat down. "What are their names?"

"Blaze is the younger one in the black hooded sweatshirt, and then Todd's in the neon green."

Just then, Blaze took a toy from another toddler.

"Blaze!" she shouted, leaning slightly over the gate.

Holding a hand up to stop her, he shook his head. "Go enjoy the service. We have it from here."

She smiled and let out a relieved sigh. "Thank you."

After service let out and after he and Lucy had cleaned the classroom, they were on their way out to the parking lot when he spotted that same woman sitting in her car, crying. Turning to his daughter, he handed her the car keys and told her to go get in the car and warm it up.

Walking over to the car window, he knocked lightly on it.

The woman rolled the window down and peered up at him. "Yeah?"

"I couldn't help but see you over here. Is everything okay?"

The window went up, then she got out of the car and shut the door.

"Since you asked, I'm going to answer. I know you don't know me, and I don't know you, but if I don't get this off my chest to someone, I might explode."

"All right." He nodded. "Go ahead."

"My sister went away to rehab last month and I agreed to watch her boys. Seems fine, right? I'm thinking okay, God. I'm not sure how this will work, but let's do it! So, I'm watching these kids. Well, it turns out these boys don't know any kind of structure at all! They're climbing counters, and they won't eat anything other than hot dogs or Pop Tarts! They hit, they destroy, they don't go to sleep. My life is *nothing* but chaos."

"Wow. Sounds hard."

"Wait." She smiled a little too wide and shook her head as she touched his arm. "It gets better. I have a job, so I'm able to escape it for a little bit each day. Turns out they get kicked out of daycare. Not once, but twice. Then . . . to top it off? Can you guess?"

15

He shrugged, not knowing what else could go wrong. "What?"

"I lost my job on Friday for missing so much work."

"*Ouch.*"

"So now I have two very dependent children, no job, and I can't even talk to my mom because she thinks it is all 'normal kid stuff' since I don't have experience in having children."

Suddenly, the woman began to cry and folded her hands over her face. She started to hyperventilate as well, causing an uneasy feeling to grow inside Brian.

Brian peered around the parking lot and then came a little closer. Uncomfortable and uneasy, he placed a hand on her back.

"It's going to be okay. It sounds really hard, but God will get you through this."

Once she calmed down, she wiped her tears from her cheeks. "How am I going to find work that allows my nephews to be there with me?"

The thought to hire her popped into Brian's mind. Then fears of it not working out followed the thought, and having the boys destroy his house didn't sound appealing. "What's your background in?"

"I worked at a dental office recently, and before that, a lot of clerical work."

He pushed his fears aside and raised an eyebrow. "I just happen to be looking to hire someone right now."

"No, you're not." She looked doubtfully at him.

"Yes, I actually am. I need someone to handle day-to-day housework and maybe some clerical work too. Emails, record keeping, and so on."

Her expression lit up. He could see hope flickering in her eyes.

Lifting a hand, Brian shook his head. "I'll warn you. A lot of people have tried to be my assistant and it hasn't worked out. I know you need a job right now, but there's a good chance it won't work. I'm a bit . . . demanding when it comes to my work and expectations."

"I'll take it! And if it doesn't work out, that's okay! I have to try something!"

Reaching in his back pocket, he pulled out his wallet and handed her a business card with his home address on it. "Come by after the kids wake up tomorrow. I'm up and working every day by five at the latest."

"Thank you!" She peered at the card. "Mr. Dunlap."

"You can call me Brian. I didn't catch your name?"

"Courtney."

"Nice to meet you, Courtney. See you tomorrow."

Walking back to his car a moment later, Brian was torn about whether he had made the right decision. Peering up at the cold, cloudless sky, he committed the matter to God. *Whatever happens, it's in Your hands, Lord.*

CHAPTER 2

COURTNEY - AGE 17

*T*he annual state fair had come to the little town of Blackfoot, Idaho, and Courtney and her sister, Taylor, were excited more so this year than usual because their father, Frank Hinley, had finally realized his dream of having a concession stand at the fair. After years of saving his and Rhonda's money, they were able to buy a local used food truck to sell homemade cooking two years ago. They had sold food out of the truck on the weekends to local businesses for the last two years and had saved enough to secure a spot at this year's state fair.

It was the night before the fair opened, and Courtney and her sister were at the fairgrounds with their parents, finishing up preparations for the next day. Grabbing the last box of homemade frozen gravy from the trunk of the car, Courtney walked the fifteen feet over to the food truck. Her sister, Taylor, had her feet kicked up on a plastic table, sipping on a cola as she reclined.

"You take it easy, Tay. I got this."

Taylor laughed and shooed a wave of one of her hands.

"Dad said I have delicate ankles, and I agree. I need to rest them."

Courtney smiled and went up the metal slatted steps into the food truck. She handed the box to her father, Frank, and he smiled at her. "Thanks, doll."

As he turned toward the deep freeze, she saw he had a small cut on his arm. "Dad. Your arm."

"Oops. A little blood there, isn't it?"

Rhonda's ears perked up at the word *blood* and came over from her work on the menu board. "Let me see that, Frank."

Turning toward her, Frank let her inspect his arm. Courtney's father had a blood clotting disorder that required him to be on a high dose of blood thinners. A gash could land him in a hospital if it was bad enough. Her mother, Rhonda, carefully looked at the wound.

"I'm not too worried. Just wrap it up and we'll keep an eye on it."

"You need to be more careful, Dad!" Taylor chided him as she entered the entryway of the truck behind Courtney.

"I know, I know. Hey. You girls take Mom's car and head home. You need your rest for tomorrow. Your mother and I will stay here and finish up getting everything ready."

"Okay. I'm driving!" Taylor spun around and darted out of the truck and toward the car. Courtney chased after her.

On their way home, they stopped at the convenience store and bought candy and soda. Then, they got home and curled up on the couch with blankets to watch a late-night talk show.

Muting the television during a commercial, Taylor turned toward Courtney.

"Are you excited for tomorrow?"

"Should be fun. I'm looking forward to earning some extra cash in life."

Taylor laughed and playfully smacked her. "I'm talking about the boys we get to meet!"

Courtney laughed and shook her head. "I don't think the husband God has for me is going to come talk to me at the fair tomorrow when I smell like food and have an inch of sweat across my forehead."

"You never know! Did I tell you I saw your old friend Chelsea over by the stadium today? I was over there getting a drink and she was with her husband. Her kids were acting like total brats! I can't believe she already has children and she's only nineteen!"

"Don't be mean. You don't know what she's going through. I wouldn't mind having children early in life."

"I know you wouldn't. You're such a weirdo!"

Courtney playfully, but with a little force, punched Taylor in the arm.

"Ouch!" Taylor slapped her with a piece of licorice.

The next morning, Courtney sipped on her cup of sugar with a splash of coffee in it as she waited for noon to roll around and business to start picking up at the food truck. As she waited, a group of guys from her graduating class of last year walked by. Peering over at her, they laughed and kept walking. She knew why they were laughing. She was wearing a ridiculous bright yellow shirt and a yellow visor. Rolling her eyes, she took another drink of her coffee and thought to herself how she was earning money while they were doing nothing.

Her mother, Rhonda, called her over to the flat top. Sizzling patties lifted an aroma that was permeating the air. "Could you keep an eye on these patties while I go find your father? He went to get ice and still hasn't found his way back."

"Yes." Watching over the patties, she turned toward her

sister who was at the cash register staring across the walkway at one of the *Giant Tom's Burgers* guys. "Do you know that guy?"

"That's Steven. He was in my Spanish class. Isn't he cute?"

Laughing, Courtney nodded. "Sure. Why haven't you guys dated?"

"You know Dad's rule."

"Hasn't stopped you before . . ."

"True, but . . . I don't know." Taylor turned toward Courtney. "It's weird, but when I know a guy is into me, I don't like them as much. He's too sweet and stuff."

"Oh, Sister." Turning back to the patties on the flat top, she saw they needed flipped. Grabbing the metal spatula from the magnetic strip on the wall, Courtney flipped the patties over.

"Customers!" Taylor excitedly clapped and adjusted her footing as a lady and child approached.

"Do you know where the restrooms are?"

Taylor pointed toward the stadium down the walkway. "Over there."

Courtney laughed. "We'll be busy soon enough."

"I hope so."

By eleven that morning, Frank and Rhonda's food truck was flinging homemade food and had a line down to the Kia dealership tent a half-mile down the walkway. Frank and Taylor ran the cash registers while Courtney and Rhonda kept the food coming. The family of four worked well together and seamlessly as they met the demand the first day at the fair. When the slow time came between lunch and dinner, Courtney took a break and went to go check out the farm animals in the barns. She knew from past fairs that the first day was the only day she could stomach seeing the animals due to the natural occurrence that happened when warm temperatures and animals' living environment mixed for prolonged periods of time.

Entering her favorite barn, where the goats were located, she smiled as she approached the first of the goats. The sounds made her laugh as she approached with a cup of feed in her hand. Holding out a hand, she let a goat eat from her palm. Without her being aware, another goat was nearby and stole the cup from her other hand.

"Hey!" Reaching through the fence, she retrieved the now empty cup from the goat's mouth. Reaching in her pocket, she realized the rest of her money was in her purse inside her mother's car. She sighed deeply.

"Here. Take mine."

Turning, she saw a guy her age standing there offering her his full cup of animal feed.

"I can't take that. It was my own fault."

"I insist. Take it."

"Thank you."

She took the cup and poured a little out onto her palm. As she fed another goat, she turned to that same guy who was now helping a little girl feed one of the sheep in the next pin over. Courtney felt obligated to say something more than 'thank you.'

"Is that your sister?"

"Niece. She loves the animals. I bring her every year." Turning toward the girl who couldn't be more than five, he smiled as he peered down at her. "She might be blind, but she can feel their love with her heart."

Courtney's heart was touched that he was so kind to bring his blind niece to the fair every year. Wanting to know more, she came closer to the two of them. "That's nice of you to bring her."

The guy shrugged. "It's the least I can do. Her parents introduced me to Jesus a few years back. It changed my life

23

forever, and I could never repay them enough for the introduction to my Savior and my salvation."

He's a Christian? The thought brought waves of excitement within her.

"You working here at the fair?" He looked her up and down and her cheeks went crimson with embarrassment as she remembered the obnoxious yellow shirt and visor she was wearing.

"Yeah. My parents run a food truck."

"That's awesome. They paying you?"

Raising her eyebrows, she relaxed and nodded. "Yes! I am trying to save up some money for a car."

"Smart." His niece started to wander and he caught sight of her. "I'd better keep going. It was nice meeting you. My name is Drew."

"Nice to meet you, Drew. My name is Courtney."

"Maybe I'll see you around."

"*Maybe.*"

The next day on her break, she went back to the barn in the hopes of finding Drew, but he wasn't there. She went again the following day and the day after that, but he wasn't there. By the end of the week, she had earned enough for a car, but she couldn't help but find herself discontented that she hadn't seen Drew again.

It wasn't until the following year when she was eighteen that she saw him again. There he was, feeding the goats with his niece once again.

It felt like a dream, seeing him again. Proceeding closer, her heart began to race. He was but a stranger whom she had shared a moment with a year ago, but he had been in her thoughts and her prayers ever since that chance meeting. Did he feel the same? She had hope.

"Drew? Is that you?"

He stood and turned toward her. It was as if it was in

slow motion. As his gaze connected with hers, his smile widened. "Courtney? I searched and searched for you last year and couldn't find you. I can't believe you're really here. I made a mistake last year by not getting your phone number. I didn't even think of it at the time. I can't let another moment go by without it. Sorry if that's too forward."

"No, not at all. I thought about you a lot too. Here." She pulled out a pen and grabbed his hand, pulling him closer to her. She wrote it down on his hand.

It turned out he lived in Idaho Falls, just twenty minutes north of Blackfoot. Over the course of the next year, they dated and fell in love, and then two years following that fateful day at the fair, they were married. She was only nineteen, but Courtney was happy and looking forward to a life with Drew.

Lying on a blanket in the grass one summer day after being married for two years, Courtney sat up and turned to Drew.

"Why do you think we haven't been able to have children?"

He sat upright and shrugged. "I'm not sure the *why*, but I do know God is in control."

"Why would God want us to not have kids?"

Drew's gaze left Courtney's eyes and went across the lawn to the large oak tree that was blowing lightly in the wind. "I don't think it's a matter of God not wanting us to have kids, love. Sometimes, things just don't happen the way we think they should happen. It's in these moments that our love and trust in God must take hold of all that we are and be at the forefront of our thoughts."

He turned his gaze back to Courtney, then leaned in and kissed her lips gently. "His loving ways are beyond our comprehension, and we must trust in Him above all else."

Nodding, Courtney lay back down on the blanket and so

did Drew. She snuggled up to his chest and wrapped her arms around him tightly. She loved his heart for God, his trust in God. She prayed quietly to herself in that moment. *I love him so much, Lord. Thank You for this man. Thank You for this husband I get to call my own.*

CHAPTER 3

Chimes rang through Brian's house early Monday morning. Peering down at the clock on his computer screen, he saw it was 6:15 AM. Scratching his head, he stood up from his office chair and tightened his robe on his way through the house. The chimes went off again. Finally opening the door, he was surprised to see Courtney and her two nephews bright-eyed and looking as if they hadn't slept for hours.

"Wow. You're here early."

"You said six AM, right?"

"Yeah, yeah. Sure, come on in." Stepping out of the way, he let them into the house. He had set an alarm on his phone to remind him to pull out some of Lucy's old toys at eight that morning. "I have a room that will work perfectly for your office and playroom."

"Playroom?" Courtney raised an eyebrow.

"Well, yeah, the kids need something to do. There's already a TV in there, and I had planned to bring out some old toys of my daughter's."

"Wow, thank you. Hey. So you own a dog food company and you don't have a dog?"

Brian laughed and shook his head. "Not anymore. Anyway, thank you for trying this out. Come with me. I'll show you to the room." Leading her and the boys through a long hallway, he led her into a giant room with giant windows overlooking the back yard. She walked over to the window and peered out.

"Wow. You have a whole lot of space." She turned toward him. "I bet Mrs. Dunlap and your children enjoy it."

Brian shook his head. "No Mrs. Dunlap . . . anymore . . . and I have one daughter who visits once a month." Walking over to the television, he turned it on and grabbed the remote from beside the entertainment stand. He handed it to her. "I'll go grab the toys. You can find something for them to watch."

Heading down the hall, he went into the study off the foyer and dug through a few boxes sitting on the writing table in the room. Pulling out dolls, he shook his head and placed them back into the box. He managed to find a few books and a small train. Setting the box aside, he grabbed another and opened it up.

Just then, Courtney entered through the open glass doors into the study. He turned toward her, looking over his shoulder with a smile. "I found a train and some books so far."

"Thank you. I'll have them bring a few of their toy cars tomorrow."

She entered the foyer and glanced at a photograph on the desk in the room. "This your ex-wife?"

"Yes."

"She's very beautiful."

"Yeah, you don't know her." He kept digging in the box but realized what he had just uttered. Stopping, he removed his hands from the box and turned toward Courtney. "That's not nice to say. It just didn't work out between us."

"Can I ask what happened?"

His heart jerked, flashbacks of his finding out about her and Conrad. "No. I'd rather not talk about it. It's too early, and it's Monday—oh, and I'm your boss."

"That's all very true, and I'm sorry." She came over to the train sitting on the desk. Lifting it, she smiled. "I'm sure Blaze will like to play with this. You aren't too attached, though, right? There's a good chance it might get broken. These boys are rough with toys—I mean, *everything*."

He laughed lightly. "That's fine."

"Honestly, I'm surprised you hired me after yesterday when I told you they were wild." She touched her forehead as she paused and shook her head. "You probably think I'm quite the mess after yesterday in the parking lot. Don't you?"

Coming closer to Courtney, Brian shook his head. "I don't think you're a mess. I think you're just going through a hard time right now. It's okay to not be okay."

She smiled. "Thank you."

Her eyes went to the box, then over to the train and books. "When are you going to show me what to do for the job?"

His mind shifted to his work and he let out a quick breath. "Let me get some more stuff done and we'll meet up around ten. Feel free to go through these boxes to find any toys that might interest your boys. Oh, and take a self-guided tour around the house so you can get a feel for your work environment."

"Okay. So, you don't want me to do any work until eleven?"

"It's whatever. Just hang out. I'll still pay you."

"All right."

Leaving her be, he headed to his office and continued his

work on the ad designs he had to get finished. Stretching his arms out as he finished the last ad at five minutes to ten o'clock, he rubbed his eyes of exhaustion and rose from his seat at the computer. Exiting his office, he headed down the hall to go find Courtney. As he passed the kitchen, he noticed it was clean and all the dishes were done. He and Lucy had dirtied it up over the weekend. Raising an eyebrow, he went into the kitchen and found a freshly brewed pot of coffee.

He poured himself a cup. "Mmm . . . this is great."

"Glad you think so." Courtney walked into the kitchen. "I took the liberty of cleaning up while I waited for eleven. I also prepared lunch and dinner, and it's ready to go when you're ready for me to cook it. I just finished starting the second load of laundry. Hope you don't mind that I took some initiative while I waited."

Tingles ran the length of Brian's spine. "Mind?" He took another sip of his coffee and set it down on the counter as his lips curled into a smile. "I love it!"

Courtney smiled. "Good. So, other than housework, what's this job all about?"

"Glad you asked. I am up to my ears in work with advertising, suppliers, meetings with clients, and running the website and warehouse where the dog food is made. I need someone to handle all the records, emails, and scheduling of appointments."

"All right. That computer in the office you gave me is slow."

"It worked great the last time I used it."

"With all due respect, it has Windows 98 on it. It's old, and also, the metal folding chair won't work for me, either."

Brian laughed and raked a hand through his hair. "98 was a great year, and that chair works for sitting."

Raising an eyebrow, she shrugged. "Probably so, but it's 2019. As for that chair, maybe we can just switch chairs for a day and you can tell me how it feels to sit on it for hours on end?"

"All right. Here." Pulling out his wallet, he handed her a credit card. "Order it."

"I'll let you handle that part."

"Why? You should start getting used to handling my finances."

She took it. "Okay, then. When the computer arrives in a couple of days, I will need you to set everything up so I have access to all that I am responsible for. Do you have hard copies of invoices as well as digitals?"

"Yeah, they're in the basement in the far-left corner." She was about to leave when he stopped her. "Hey, Courtney. I have to say I'm impressed and a little surprised. I hope you don't mind my asking, but where'd all this energy come from? You seem different."

"It's no offense to me, and I'm glad you're impressed. As for the change? When I work, I work hard and I'm focused."

"Awesome."

She headed for the door that led to the basement. Raising an eyebrow, he nodded and headed back to his office. Brian already knew just a few hours into her first day that she wasn't like the rest of the people he had tried out for the position of assistant. Courtney didn't feel comfortable getting paid to do nothing and took initiative, and he liked that.

BRINGING UP THE FINAL BOX of invoices, she set them down in the office and noticed the boys were growing bored of the few books and train that Brian had supplied. They were wrestling with each other near the window. Breaking up the tussle, Courtney asked if they wanted to watch a movie.

"I'm hungry." Todd ran over to her purse sitting on the couch in the room.

"Okay. You can have a small snack. It's about that time." Walking over to her purse, she retrieved two packages of an assortment of grapes and crackers. Handing them to Todd and Blaze, she watched as Todd threw his bag across the floor. Blaze, however, started popping grapes into his mouth.

Praying as she grabbed the bag from the floor, Courtney knew she needed the Lord's strength today. *Please help him to listen, Lord. Please!*

Dropping to a knee in front of the angered Todd, she gently brought a hand up to press against his back as she peered into his eyes. "Honey. This is your snack."

"I don't like grapes or crackers. I want candy."

Shaking her head, she smiled. "I know, but this is healthier for you."

"No. I'm not eating it." He jerked his body away from her and stood with furrowed eyebrows directing his attention away from her. Her heart ached in the moment. Placing the bag back into her purse, she stood up and walked over to the couch. She set the purse down.

"If you get hungry, let me know and you can have your snack. Let's go for our walk and stretch our legs." She had read an article that walking helps children calm down. Reaching a hand out, she waited.

He stayed looking away from her.

Glancing over at Blaze, she saw that he was done with his snack and ready to go.

"Come on, Todd. Let's go." Walking over to him, she offered her hand again.

He reluctantly took it and went with her and Blaze for a walk.

COURTNEY WAS ONE WEEK INTO her new job and everything was going smoothly. She had almost all seven boxes of invoices organized by months and years into a filing cabinet in her office. His email inbox was to under forty emails, down from over twelve hundred, and his house was clean and tidy. The boys were behaving for the most part at Brian's house, and Courtney had finally felt like she had some control over her life for the first time in a little over a month since her sister went to rehab in Wyoming.

One evening, after tucking the boys into their new toddler beds in the spare bedroom, she switched the night light on and shut the door. Pausing outside the door, she sat down and waited, back resting against the hallway wall. Each night she put them to bed, she had to wait by the door and coax them back into their bedroom several times until they finally passed out around ten or eleven, hours after she had put them to bed.

Tonight, they didn't get up.

Hot tears filled her eyes as joy poured into her heart. It had been a trying and difficult five weeks since she'd started the process of bedtime after their mother left, but they had finally learned bedtime meant bedtime. She wanted to call and celebrate the victory with someone, but she didn't know who to call. Her mother wouldn't care since she'd tried telling her to play a movie for them like they were used to and her sister was busy fighting addiction. Then she thought of Brian. She called him.

"Hello, Courtney. What's up?"

"I had to call someone, and I think you'd understand it best since you know the boys. They went to sleep without getting up at all tonight."

"What?" He was elated. "That is fantastic! What an awesome victory for you!"

"I know! I'm so excited."

"Your mother wouldn't be excited about this?"

"Nah. She thinks everything that goes on with them is *normal* kid stuff. I don't think she cares a whole lot. She couldn't even be bothered to come to town for Thanksgiving last week, so . . ."

"Ah, yeah. Well, you should pray for her. I take it she hasn't seen Todd in one of his full-on meltdowns like the one I saw in the kitchen the other day."

"Nope. He's perfect on video chat and that's all she ever sees. I will pray for her. That's a good idea."

"Good plan. Hey, I forgot to tell you earlier today when you were here. Great job with Paula Erickson. She wrote a fabulous review on Facebook about us, gushing over the customer service experience she had when dealing with the order mix-up she had from the warehouse."

Courtney's heart warmed. "Wow, that's awesome, Brian! I'm glad I am of some use."

"Hey." He paused for a moment. "You're a great asset to *Puppy Chow Direct* and to me. You've made my life so much easier to manage, and it is a huge blessing to have you as a part of the team! I know it's only been a week, but it's been great. You've been great."

"Aw, thanks."

"No problem. Have a good night, Courtney. I'll see you tomorrow."

"See you tomorrow, Brian."

Hanging up, Courtney's eyes moistened with tears again. This time, it was thankfulness toward God for sending the perfect job into her life at the exact right time she needed it. Standing up, she opened the boys' door and peeked in at her sleeping angels. They were sound asleep, Blaze's breathing heavy and loud while Todd's breathing was silent. Her voice was but a whisper and a stray tear fell from the corner of her eye. "I love you both so much."

Closing the door, she went down the hallway and out into the living room. As she sat down on the couch, she pulled out her Bible and continued her daily reading in 2 Corinthians 4.

But we have this treasure in jars of clay to show that this all-surpassing power is from God and not from us.
We are hard pressed on every side, but not crushed; perplexed, but not in despair; persecuted, but not abandoned; struck down, but not destroyed.
We always carry around in our body the death of Jesus, so that the life of Jesus may also be revealed in our body.
2 Corinthians 4:7-10

Pausing as she finished the chapter, she peered up at the ceiling and thought of all the hardships she had endured over the last month with the boys. She knew she wasn't done with the hardships, but she was still basking in the small victory she had earlier at bedtime. She thought of Drew and how he would've been right there with her celebrating. She smiled and prayed out loud. "God, You are so good. Your power is on full display through these boys coming to live with me until Taylor gets out of rehab. It's through Your amazing grace and mercy that they are here. It's through Your power I am able to press forward and not fold under the difficulty. I know there are still two more months to go, but I already know it's going to be okay. Just like Abraham who stepped out in faith and trusted in You, I will continue to trust and continue to have faith as I watch as You work. Thank You for not giving me what I want but giving me what I need. Your kindness continues to amaze me. I love You. Amen."

Rising from the couch, she put on a kettle of water in the

kitchen for tea and looked at a photo she had of herself and Drew on the fridge. She smiled as she peered into his big brown eyes and recalled the day the photograph was taken. It was at the Blackfoot Fair on their second time ever seeing each other. She recalled how it felt to see him again after thinking she'd lost him forever. The electricity that filled every fiber of her being that day was unlike anything she ever had experienced or would experience again in her life. Then her thoughts drifted to Brian, how it felt when he picked up the phone earlier that night.

The whistle on the kettle blew, pulling her out of her thoughts.

Pouring the hot steaming water into her mug, she let her tea steep as her mind wandered to Brian again. *Why'd it feel so good when he answered?* she wondered. He was her boss, but he was also attractive and charming and provided her with an income when she needed it most. Warmth radiated in her chest as she recalled three days ago when she caught a glimpse of him walking out of his workout room without a shirt on. His muscles were ripped and sweat poured off his forehead and body.

Taking her cup of hot tea, she went into the living room and sat down. Her breath shortened as a sinking feeling of betrayal set within her. *What would Drew think?* she wondered. *He wouldn't want me being drawn to another man.* As she sipped on her tea, she began to pray to God about the emotions she felt stirring within her toward Brian. "God . . . Brian is kind and sweet, and he reminds me so much of the way Drew was, Lord. But I don't feel right about having feelings for him. What should I do?"

Silence permeated the living room. Turning her gaze toward the Bible, she thought of God's Word. It was the mouthpiece in which He spoke to His people. She knew her marriage vows were until death, so why did she feel like it was a betrayal to have feelings for another man?

At church the following Sunday, after service let out, she went up to the pastor who was shaking hands with people as they left the sanctuary.

"Pastor Matt?"

"Yes?"

"I was wondering. My husband died four years ago, and I'm feeling like I'm ready to move on, but I feel a sense of betrayal inside me with that. Why is that?"

"That's natural and normal. You see that woman over there?" He directed his gaze toward an older blonde lady who was speaking with others in the foyer. "That's Susan Lancaster. She heads the women's ministry here at the church. She's the one who can really talk to you more in-depth about it from a place of experience."

"Thank you."

"You're welcome."

Walking over to the woman, Courtney lifted a prayer asking God to give her an opportunity to get a word in before it was too late and she had to pick up the boys from Sunday school class with Brian. Upon her arrival at the people crowded around Susan, they all had finished talking to her right then and were leaving her.

Raising her eyebrows, Susan smiled. "Hello. I don't believe we've met."

"We haven't." Teary-eyed, Courtney hurried and wiped the tears from her eyes. "I lost my husband a few years ago and Pastor Matt said you might be able to help me."

"Oh, sweetie, I'm so sorry for your loss." Susan stepped closer and wrapped her arms around Courtney immediately. Holding her for a long moment, she spoke love into her. "You're so young to lose a spouse. Come sit with me for a moment."

"I have to get my boys."

"Hold on." Pulling out her cell phone from her purse, Susan called someone right there in front of Courtney. "Hey, Brian. I'm speaking with Courtney for a moment, so please don't get upset when she isn't there to get her boys right away." She paused for a moment then thanked him and hung up. Smiling at Courtney, she nodded. "There, we have time now."

Susan led Courtney over to a blue plush couch in the foyer of the church and they sat down together. Courtney told her about what was going on without using Brian's name.

"Oh, honey. It is entirely normal to feel like you are betraying your husband. You loved him dearly, I'm sure."

"Yes. He was amazing."

Susan nodded, her eyes closing slightly as she did. "My child, you are young. Was your husband a godly man?"

"Very much so."

Patting her knee, Susan nodded. "He would want you to remarry then. Think about it. Do you think he'd want you to be miserable your entire life? To never love again? Was he selfish?"

"No, he wasn't selfish. In fact . . . he wrote a letter to me in the event that he died. He told me to remarry. I just don't like feeling like I am betraying him."

"That will lessen in time, my dear."

"Yeah? How?"

"You will come to realize that he will never be replaced. What you had with him was between you and him and God. Nobody else. That isn't replaced by a new man, but instead, it's a memory that you will take with you wherever you go in life."

"I never thought of it like that . . ." Courtney thought

about telling Brian how she felt. "Should I tell my boss how I feel?"

"That's a decision you have to make. I cannot make that for you."

"Well, thank you for your time." Rising from the couch, Courtney was about to leave to get the boys when Susan touched her arm, stopping her. "You should come to my ladies' group."

She shrugged. "I don't have anyone who can watch the boys."

"Childcare can be provided. Friendships are vitally important in any Christian's life."

Raising an eyebrow, she nodded. "In that case, I'd love to go. When is it?"

"Thursday nights at seven o'clock at my house here." Walking over to a small table in the foyer, Susan picked up an informational card on the small group and handed it to her. "We'll be seeing you there this Thursday."

"Absolutely."

Arriving at the Sunday school classroom to pick up the boys, she noted that Brian didn't ask questions about her meeting with Susan. Instead, he complimented Blaze's ability to sit still during snack time.

"He's really coming along. Both of them, really."

She smiled as she lifted both boys over the gate. "Thanks. Remember, you have that meeting with the Costco rep tomorrow at eight."

"That's right. I almost forgot. Thank you."

"You're welcome. See you in the morning. We'll be there before you leave, probably."

"Sounds good! See you then."

Parking at Costco the next morning, Brian was a few minutes early and decided to review his notes and the data he had brought. Courtney had printed and organized the information for him that morning. Upon opening the folder, he found a small sticky note attached to the front page.

The boys and I are praying for you!

-Courtney

He smiled as he pulled the sticky note off and stuck it to his dashboard. Continuing to study his notes for the meeting, he carefully went over every piece of data. If he could successfully convince Costco to carry his line of dog food, operations would move from his little warehouse on Sprague to a much larger facility. It could be a game changer. After he finished looking over the notes, he bowed his head and prayed.

"God, if Costco is part of Your will for this company, let today's meeting go well. If it is not, take it away and let it slip from my fingers. If You aren't a part of it, I want nothing to do with it. I seek only to please You in all that I do. Amen."

Peering at the sticky note, he smiled again and added one more line to his prayer. "Thank you for sending Courtney and those boys into my life. Amen."

After the meeting and with no inclination in either direction from Mario, the Costco representative he met with,

Brian stopped in at the warehouse for a quick visit then headed back to his house on the South Hill.

Upon entering his house, he hung up his coat in the closet and went to find Courtney. She was in the kitchen preparing brunch. The island in the kitchen contained an assortment of sliced fruit, yogurt, freshly baked ham, eggs, and toast.

"Wow. You went all out on this meal."

Closing the fridge door, she smiled as she brought over sparkling cider and two glasses in hand. Pouring one for him, and then herself, she gave him a glass. "I figured we'd be celebrating."

Taking the glass from her, he held his grin as he raised his eyebrows. "I'm not sure if there's reason to celebrate. I won't know anything for a week or two."

"Oh, really? I'm so sorry I got the sparkling cider out! Here." She reached for the glass, but he pulled it out of her reach. "Hey, now. We can still celebrate."

She raised an eyebrow. "Yeah? What are we celebrating?"

"That we pitched Costco. God's will is going to happen no matter what they decide."

Her eyebrows lifted, smiling as they did.

"What are you smiling about?"

"Nothing."

"Come on. You can tell me."

"I just admire your faith and trust in God. It reminds me of someone . . ."

"Drew?"

She smiled and nodded gently. "Yeah. Drew."

"From everything you've told me about your husband, he sounds like he was a lucky man." Coming closer, he lifted his glass of sparkling cider. "Shall we toast?"

"Yes. To God's will."

"To God's will."

The glasses clanked together. As Brian took a drink of his

sparkling cider, he couldn't stop smiling. Not only had this beautiful woman come into his life, but she had made everything a lot easier for him. He was quickly becoming attached to the idea of having her around. As he lowered his glass down, he kept his gaze on her and placed the glass on the counter.

"Can I just say something honestly?"

She nodded.

"I am so thankful to God for your being here." He sensed his own growing affections and reminded himself that she was his employee. Fearful, he added. "You have truly fit into the role of my assistant."

Courtney smiled. "I'm glad it's working out for both of us." Walking into the other room, she called for the boys to join them in the kitchen.

CHAPTER 4

BRIAN - AGE 25

Flipping the burgers over on top of the grill, Brian shut the lid of the barbecue and turned toward the back yard. His wife, Melissa, was pushing Lucy on the swing set. When her gaze caught his, he smiled. In his heart, he lifted a prayer of thankfulness up to the Lord for his wife, his daughter, and his life. Soon, his new business he was starting with his friend selling dog food out of the garage would be operational. He and his best friend, Conrad, had come up with the brilliant idea of making their own organic dog food and selling it online. Melissa had been so supportive of the idea that she even suggested selling the house to move into their current smaller one in order to get the start-up funds needed for the venture. Everything in his life was perfect.

Melissa strolled through the grass over to Brian as he stood near the barbecue. Smiling all the way up to him, she came in close and kissed him on the lips.

"This house is really working out for us. I like the homey feeling to it."

Brian laughed. "You mean the wood paneling in the living room?"

Laughing, she playfully smacked him and then came in close, wrapping her arms around his torso. "It's fine for now."

His gaze fell back to the swing set and his daughter, Lucy. She was growing up so fast, almost five years old and starting kindergarten next month. Brian didn't know everything there was to know in the world, but he did know one thing. He knew that he loved that little girl and would fight the world for her if he had to. He prayed every day for her, and for her future husband. He often wondered what that little boy was up to. If he was playing in the mud or racing his Hot Wheels across a kitchen floor somewhere in the world.

His daughter jumped off the swing and came darting over to the two of them. "Daddy! Daddy! Did you see how high I jumped?"

Bending a knee, he smoothed a hand over her head. "Yes, I did, Princess. It was *so* high."

"Think I can go higher?"

"I think the only limit to how high you can go is you."

Her eyes flickered with youthful excitement.

Melissa turned on the radio outside and the song *Butterfly Kisses* started to play. Lucy grabbed one of Brian's hands. "Can we dance?"

"Absolutely." Scooping her up into his arms, he started to sway with her. Every time they heard the song, they'd dance no matter the occasion or what was going on. It started when she was two, and it had carried on at least yearly ever since.

A short while later, the song ended and she darted from his arms and back over to the swing, their golden retriever, Chuck, following behind her. As Brian turned toward Melissa, she raised an eyebrow.

"What time is Conrad going to be here?"

"I'm not sure. He and Alissa had another fight. He will be here soon, I'm guessing."

"*Oh*. That's concerning. I hope everything is okay. Alissa is great."

"I think the business stuff is just getting to her." Pulling Melissa closer to him, Brian smiled. "She's not as awesome as you are when it comes to all this stuff."

She smiled and kissed him. "Not everyone can be like me."

Winking, she peeled away from Brian and headed inside.

After dinner that evening, Brian and Conrad went out to the garage, headquarters for *Puppy Chow Direct*. Flipping on the light switch as they entered, Brian glanced around. They had converted the garage into a full-sized kitchen to create their organic dog food to be frozen and then shipped out.

"Man, it's really here. We'll be operational in less than a month." Conrad smiled as he walked over to the stacks of containers containing the nutrients they added to each batch of food. "Did the vet nutritionist sign off on the final blend after we tweaked it?"

"Yes." Bending a knee as his dog came over to him, Brian began to pet him. "She came by yesterday."

"Nice. Any new feedback from early reviewers on the dog food?"

"Yeah, the dogs all love it." Brian stood and walked over to one of the metal chairs in the room. Staring at his friend as he took a seat, he sighed. "Conrad?"

"What?" He turned toward Brian, letting his hand fall away from the container it was touching.

"What's going on with you and Alissa? You haven't said anything about it all night."

Raking his hand through his hair, he shook his head and walked over to Brian. Sitting down in the chair beside him, he turned toward him. "We're not in love anymore."

"What?" Brian adjusted in his chair. "What does that even mean? Love is a choice."

"Sometimes, it's not a choice, Brian. I know everything is black and white for you, but it isn't for everyone." Standing up, Conrad walked over to the ovens and leaned against them as he crossed his arms. "She doesn't love me anymore, and I don't think I love her anymore."

Brian's chest tightened and he stood up. Walking over to Conrad, he shook his head. "That's your wife. You have to fight for your marriage."

"She's seeing someone already, man. I don't want the drama or the fight. I need to focus on this business and what we have going on here."

Brian's face softened as his heart broke for his friend. "She's seeing someone?"

"Yeah."

Brian couldn't ever fathom what that'd feel like, nor did he want to experience it firsthand. "That's rough. Just know I'm praying for you, brother."

Releasing his folded arms, Conrad rested a hand on Brian's shoulder. "Thank you. You and Melissa are amazing friends, and I hope that doesn't stop just because Alissa and I don't work out. You know?"

"We're business partners. That's not going to change."

Conrad smiled somberly. "Thanks, man."

The first four months of business were bleak for Brian and Conrad. They could barely give the dog food away, let alone sell it. They were working long hours in the garage and working every weekend in the hopes of finding the magic bullet they needed to get the product to take off. With funds dwindling and hope running out, Brian took a trip to Florida to pitch the product to a small company that had a chain of pet stores. They were interested in the product after they had tested out the sample with their own dog, Skippy, and they wanted to hear what *Puppy Chow Direct* could offer.

The meeting had taken one day instead of two, and Brian took it upon himself to return home early to surprise his wife and Conrad with the great news of being picked up by the small chain of pet stores. When he pulled into the driveway and saw Conrad's car parked out front, he thought nothing of it, thinking he was busy working in the garage.

What followed would be the most difficult experience of Brian's life. Instead of turning away from God, he turned more toward God than ever. Melissa ended up leaving him and marrying Conrad the year following their divorce. Conrad was willing to be bought out of his share in the company and went on to work as a restaurant supply consultant.

Hurt by what the two of them had done, Brian dedicated himself to God and the operations of the business, swearing off women and relationships from that point moving forward.

CHAPTER 5

On a cold morning in early December, Courtney pulled up behind an unfamiliar car in the round-about gravel driveway at Brian's house. It was a black SUV. Peering through her windshield as she shut the car off, she saw a man standing and talking to Brian at the doorway. Brian didn't look pleased to be in the conversation with the individual.

"Momma." Blaze's voice lifted from the back seat.

"Auntie." Her attempts to correct Blaze and Todd on calling her Mom didn't seem to prevent the occasional slip-ups. They both regularly called her it, though she resolved that it was just a natural part of her caring for them. Her sister feared the boys forgetting who she was, and that was the furthest desire from Courtney's mind, so she made sure to correct them each time it happened. She only had a little over a month left before Taylor would be coming back into their lives, and they needed to know their real mother was her, not Courtney. While she loved them both to pieces, she was counting the days they would be back in Taylor's care.

Unbuckling the kids from their car seats, she traveled up

the light snow-dusted gravel driveway toward the steps, passing the stranger as they did. He smiled and nodded but said nothing on his way to his vehicle.

Coming up the steps, Courtney saw the soured look on Brian's face and glanced toward the SUV once more.

"Solicitor?"

"No. My ex-wife's husband, Conrad."

"You don't like him, I take it?"

Forcing a smile, he shook his head. "I've been trying to pray that root of bitterness out from my heart for a while now. Come on inside."

As she shut the door behind her inside the foyer, the kids ran off toward the playroom. Courtney turned toward Brian. "Want to talk about it?"

"I'm okay. Hey. My daughter is here today. Your boys should be good with her. Right?"

Raising her eyebrows as she opened the coat closet and hung up her coat, she glanced over her shoulder at him. "Yes. Why? You need me for something?"

"Yes. I rented a trailer, and I need help loading it with some old equipment from one of the garages. It's stuff from when we first started the business. Just need to get it hauled off."

She shrugged. "I don't know how much help I'll be, but I'll try to help!"

"Sounds good. Let me introduce you and the boys to my daughter, and then give me fifteen minutes or so to finish up a Costco display mockup I'm working on and I'll meet you out at the garages."

He called for Lucy and she came into the foyer from the kitchen.

"Yes, Dad?" Her eyes went immediately to Courtney. "Who's this? The woman you hired?"

Adjusting her footing, Courtney felt uneasy by the look Lucy flashed her direction.

"Yes, this is Courtney. Courtney, this is my daughter, Lucy."

They shook hands.

"Courtney's two boys I told you about are down in the last room on the left."

"Okay . . ." Lucy shrugged, a puzzled look on her face.

"Why are you acting like that? Come here for a moment." Brian took his daughter into the kitchen out of earshot from Courtney. More unsettling waves rose within Courtney as she stood waiting for the two of them. Why didn't his daughter like her? Could Lucy somehow detect Courtney's affections toward Brian? She tried to push all of her thoughts away from the matter and focus on the fact that she was an employee, even though her heart was gravitating toward something more.

A moment later, the two of them returned.

Lucy apologized. "I'm sorry I was rude before. I didn't mean to be. Can I meet your boys?"

"Yeah, let's do that."

Brian lightly touched Courtney's arm. "I'll catch up with you out at the garage in a little bit."

"Okay."

Walking with Lucy, Courtney attempted to make small talk with her. "How's school? You excited for winter break coming up?"

"It's fine. Yes." Lucy stopped in the hallway before they made it to the office. Turning, she looked down the hallway, appearing to make sure her father wasn't around, then looked back at Courtney. "Listen, I love my dad and I don't want him to get hurt. You seem like a nice lady and all, but he's really sweet and unavailable for dating."

Shaking her head, Courtney smiled. "I just work for your dad."

Lucy looked at the floor for a moment, then back at her. "I saw the way he looked at you. It was just like how he used to look at Mom when they were still married. I don't remember lots from when I was younger, but I remember that."

Courtney's heart melted at hearing the revelation. "*Oh?*"

Just then, the boys came out into the hallway. Todd was jumping up and down as he pointed toward the open office doorway. "Come look at this car go really fast on the floor!"

"Excuse me." Courtney took the opportunity to slip away from the conversation with Brian's daughter.

After introductions with the boys and Lucy, Courtney found her way outside to the open garage, one of three, and the trailer on the far western side of the property. The cold winter air was crisp. The day's weather forecast called for snow later that morning that was supposed to stretch into part of the afternoon. Arriving inside the garage, she saw stacks of random kitchen equipment, ovens, microwaves, and stove tops all stacked in a corner of the open bay. There was also a large pile of mixing bowls, pots and pans, and random odds and ends.

Courtney stood for a few minutes waiting, then caught sight of a door connected to the next garage bay. Curious, she walked over to the door and turned the knob. It was unlocked. She went in and flipped on the light switch.

Boxes filled the floor space. One was tipped over and a photograph was sitting on the floor. She picked it up and looked at it. It was a photograph of Brian and his ex-wife and their daughter from years ago. They were standing in front of a far smaller house than the one Brian lived in. Peering at Brian's face, she saw something she didn't see much of —happiness.

"Got bored?" Brian's voice startled her.

Whipping around, she smiled and handed him the photograph. "It was on the floor by that tipped over box."

"Ahh." He glanced at the photograph and then went over to the box and set it upright. Tossing it into the box, he closed it. "That was the house Melissa and I moved into after we sold our nice one. We moved so we had the funds to start the business." He laughed, shaking his head. "Months later, she cheated on me with my business partner and then left me for him."

Courtney's heart ached in the moment as the puzzle pieces were coming together in her mind. "Conrad."

Walking over to the door, he motioned with a hand. "Let's get to work. We have a lot to do today."

AFTER DROPPING OFF THE EQUIPMENT at a Salvation Army thrift store, Brian stopped and got hot cocoas for the children and coffee for himself and Courtney. When he arrived back at the house, he was pleasantly surprised to find his daughter reading to the boys in the living room on the couch. It was refreshing to see her not on her cell phone, scrolling through social media.

"Come into the kitchen. I have a surprise for you all."

Lucy jumped up, along with the boys from the couch, and they all went into the kitchen.

"Oh, sweet! I was just thinking about some hot cocoa this morning!" Lucy grabbed two cups and helped get the boys situated at the kitchen island on stools. Then she sat with them and grabbed her own cup. It pleased his heart to see his daughter so friendly and helpful with the boys.

Taking his and Courtney's coffee in his hands, he traveled down the hallway to Courtney's office. As he walked in, she lifted her gaze and turned toward him, smiling as her eyes fell on the coffees.

"Coffees?"

"Yes. A token of my gratitude for your help this morning with the equipment." He walked over and handed her the coffee.

She laughed lightly and took a sip. Peering at him, she shook her head. "You pay me. I thought that was a token of gratitude."

He laughed. "I guess I do pay you, but thanks, anyway. Moving kitchen equipment was never part of the job description."

Courtney stood up and nodded. "True, but I didn't mind. It was nice."

Walking over to the windows overlooking the back yard, she looked out at the falling snow. "I love snow when it first shows up. It's so beautiful as it blankets everything."

Without control, Brian thought in his heart, *you're beautiful.* Brian's affections for Courtney were growing a little more every day, but he was her employer. Plus, he didn't want to get himself tangled up in a relationship. He had been hurt before by getting his heart involved, and he couldn't risk the pain of it again. Yet, he couldn't stop from feeling more for this woman. She worked hard, made his life easier, had a beautiful and godly perspective, and most of all, she had a heart he admired.

Joining her at the window, he looked out as the snow fell from the sky and covered every part of the yard.

Glancing at him, she raised an eyebrow. "Did you know each snowflake is unique?"

"Yes, I've heard that before." He took a deep drink of his coffee. As he stood by her side and peered out to the back yard, his heart radiated warmth and everything felt right in that moment. He could smell the perfume she was wearing. It was the same smell he caught a whiff of earlier that morning and every day he saw her. It was quickly becoming a smell that made him feel more relaxed, more comfortable, more at ease. It had only been a month since she entered his life, but she was quickly an addiction and he only wanted more of her. He pushed against the desires and took a step back from the window and her. "I'd better get back to work."

He turned and started to leave the office. As he made it to the door to leave, Courtney called out to him.

"Would you mind if I took a break and made salt dough ornaments with all the kids?"

Raising an eyebrow, he turned back toward her. "That's a good idea." He paused, his desire to be near her growing in intensity. "Could I join you?"

Her soft pink lips curled up on both sides. "I'd like that."

The kids were soon back to reading with Lucy in the living room as Brian and Courtney made the salt dough for the ornaments. Seeing Courtney grow weary of kneading the dough, he came over and tried to take over. When she resisted, he couldn't help but place his hands atop hers, thinking she would move. She didn't. Instead, she smiled and flashed a look at him that melted the coldest part of his heart. He kept his eyes locked on her eyes. "I'll take it from here."

She shook her head. "No." Clearing her throat, she brought the volume of her voice up a notch. "Take that 'I'm in charge' attitude out of my kitchen. I'm getting paid to do this, so let me handle it."

He shook his head and smiled as he thrust his hips sideways to playfully push her out of the way. "You're obviously tired. I got this, Courtney."

Laughing, she stumbled slightly and moved out of his way. Resting a hand on her hip, she watched him meticulously as he kneaded. "You're doing it wrong. You see, Brian? You can't do *everything*."

"No, I'm not doing it wrong." Brian looked at the dough and pushed his hands firmly into it.

Coming over to him, she shoved her hip into his and took back over the kneading. She worked the dough, pushing with her palms.

A strand of hair fell into her eyes, and she blew it up and out of the way as her gaze met his again. "You have to get your palms into it."

He came close and wrapped his arms around her, his insides trembling as he placed his hands on the dough, folding it over. "Like this?"

She stopped and turned toward him, their faces a mere six inches from each other. Her voice was soft. "Yeah. Like that."

"Mommy?" Blaze's voice interrupted the moment, and Brian leapt backward, his back hitting the fridge.

"Yes, Blaze?" Her gaze was fixed on him. "It's Auntie, but go on."

"I miss Tay."

"You miss Mommy, you mean." Walking over to him, she got down on her knees and spoke to him delicately as she brushed his hair back. "Your mom is getting better so she can take care of you. Just a little while longer and you'll see her again. I promise. Thirty-four more days, bud!"

"Tomorrow?"

She leaned forward and hugged Blaze. "Soon, baby. Soon."

After Blaze left the room, she kept glancing toward the doorway he exited through. "He's so sweet and tender. I hope she gets better for good. You know?"

Brian nodded, a part of him wondering if that moment before Blaze walked in could be recaptured. He set it aside and focused on Courtney and her words.

"It's going to be hard for you to let them go, isn't it?"

Her eyes moistened as she nodded. Wiping the tears from

her cheeks as they fell, she shrugged. "But at least I got to love on them for a little while. You know?"

"That's an amazing kind of love to have for them. You're such a good motherly figure to them."

She laughed and shook her head. "You don't see me when it's just me and them." Her eyebrows went up as she continued shaking her head. "I can get pretty angry on occasion."

"I'm sure, but . . . you love them. It's easy to see that."

Courtney looked at Brian in that moment with another look he could feel down deep in the depths of his soul.

"Yes, I do."

Brian's head caught up with the situation and reminded him of Melissa. Would Courtney break his heart just like Melissa did? Uneasiness rose inside him like flood waters as he didn't have a sure answer to that question. Melissa had seemed genuine, perfect, and loving, yet she did the most hurt and damage to his heart. Courtney could do the same.

"Let me know when the kids are painting the ornaments and I'll rejoin you all. I spaced on this thing I have to get done today."

"Okay." Courtney nodded in agreement. "I'll come get you."

"Great."

Getting down the hall and to his office, he went and shut the door. His breath was short and he peered up at the ceiling and prayed. "God . . . what am I doing? This is my employee. I don't even know where her heart truly lies. It could just be a ploy to get more money. Help me."

Raking a hand through his hair, he went over to his office chair and sat down. Pulling out the Bible he kept in a drawer in his office, he opened it up and began to read in John 13.

It was just before the Passover Festival. Jesus knew that the hour had come for him to leave this world and go to the Father. Having loved his own who were in the world, he loved them to the end.

The evening meal was in progress, and the devil had already prompted Judas, the son of Simon Iscariot, to betray Jesus.

Jesus knew that the Father had put all things under his power, and that he had come from God and was returning to God;

so he got up from the meal, took off his outer clothing, and wrapped a towel around his waist.

After that, he poured water into a basin and began to wash his disciples' feet, drying them with the towel that was wrapped around him.

He came to Simon Peter, who said to him, "Lord, are you going to wash my feet?"

Jesus replied, "You do not realize now what I am doing, but later you will understand."

"No," said Peter, "you shall never wash my feet."

Jesus answered, "Unless I wash you, you have no part with me."

"Then, Lord," Simon Peter replied, "not just my feet but my hands and my head as well!"

Jesus answered, "Those who have had a bath need only to wash their feet; their whole body is clean.

And you are clean, though not every one of you."

For he knew who was going to betray him, and that was why he said not every one was clean.

When he had finished washing their feet, he put on his clothes and returned to his place.

"Do you understand what I have done for you?" he asked them.

"You call me 'Teacher' and 'Lord,' and rightly so, for that is what I am.

Now that I, your Lord and Teacher, have washed your feet, you also should wash one another's feet.

I have set you an example that you should do as I have done for you.

Very truly I tell you, no servant is greater than his master,
nor is a messenger greater than the one who sent him.
Now that you know these things, you will be blessed if you do them.
John 13:1-17

The tension binding Brian's heart loosened after he finished the story. Jesus had only hours left before he'd be given over to the authorities, and what did He do? He served, He washed their feet. Brian's heart clung to the example that Jesus, his Lord and Savior, had set before him in the passage. Jesus could've been upset and worried about the coming trial and difficulty. He could've been concerned over the painful physical and emotional turmoil that He would endure, but He wasn't focused on that. He was focused on *loving them until the end.*

Turning his gaze toward his office door, he thought about Courtney. Thought about his ex-wife, Melissa. Courtney could betray him, that was true. She could very well drag him through the mud and break his heart just like Melissa had done to him. Brian had a decision to make. Was he going to walk in the footsteps of Jesus and love others until the end? Or let the past hold him back? Even knowing the pain would come, his Savior set an example for Brian to follow.

Brian exited the office a few minutes later and went to his bedroom to change into workout clothes. Crossing by the kitchen entryway on his way to work, he stopped in.

He caught Courtney's attention. "I'm hitting the treadmill and weights for a bit. How are we looking on time?"

"Still a bit. I forgot to preheat the oven. Should be plenty of time for your workout."

"Great. Thanks."

Continuing down to the workout room, he went in and

shut the door behind him. Cranking up the stereo, he grabbed a hand towel and draped it over the weight bench. Stepping onto the treadmill, he hit the *Go* button and started his jog.

As he jogged, he focused his mind on the music. *Oh, my soul . . .*

Cranking up the speed on the treadmill after a five-minute warmup, he started to do sprints of five minutes, then two-minute cooldowns. His endurance had been getting better since he dusted off the equipment two months ago, shortly after Courtney started working for him.

When he finally stopped the jog, sweat poured from every surface of his body. He forced his weak legs over to the bench and sat down, patting his face with the towel. As his breathing slowed, one thought permeated his mind more than any other thought. *What am I going to do about Courtney?*

BRIAN KEPT HIS DISTANCE THROUGHOUT the rest of the day Courtney was at the house. During the painting portion of the salt dough ornaments, he stayed opposite of her in the kitchen, keeping the oversized granite kitchen island between them. She knew he felt something, just like she did earlier that day, and she concluded that was the reason for his distance.

When she was leaving that evening around six thirty, Brian emerged from the front door of his house in his sweats and a T-shirt. He ran down the steps and toward her car as she buckled Todd and Blaze into their car seats. Shutting the back door of the car, she met him in front of the car's head-lights as the snow continued to fall.

"What's up?"

"I just wanted to talk to you for a moment."

"We've been together all day. What do you mean? You had all day."

He glanced behind him at the front door, then at the car. "I meant alone. Listen."

"Okay."

He took a step closer to her, sending her pulse skyrocketing. "I sense something between us, Courtney. I don't know if you do, and if you don't ever want to come back here, I understand and will pay a severance. I know I'm your boss, and I don't want you to feel obligated to—"

Courtney smiled and placed a finger on his lips. "Shh. I feel the same way about you."

Brian smiled and raised his eyebrows. "Really?"

"Yes. But I don't think your daughter likes the idea of an *us*."

Shaking his head, he glanced over his shoulder for a moment, then his gaze met Courtney's again. "Don't worry about her. We don't need to tell her until we know where this is going. Right?"

"Yeah. That's a good idea. So, how will this work? It's kind of complicated since you're my boss."

"That's easy. You're fired."

Her heart dipped and she raised her eyebrows. "What?"

Laughing, he shooed his hand through the air. "I'm just kidding!"

Playfully smacking his shoulder, she shook her head as she grinned. "Not funny!"

"You just keep working for me and we'll see where things go?"

"All right."

"Sweet." Rubbing his bare arms to recapture the warmth, he shifted himself toward the house. "I'd better get back inside. I'll see you Sunday?"

"See you Sunday!"

She got into her car and watched as Brian hurried up the steps and into his house. As the door shut, she smiled and thought about the two of them. She had already dreamed of him kissing her on several occasions since starting her job, but she'd never thought it could possibly happen. On her drive home that evening, she prayed the whole way home about the situation. While part of her was apprehensive about dating her boss, she couldn't help but think that maybe this was all part of God's plan.

As she pulled into her parking stall at the apartment, she noticed her apartment's lights on inside. Her heart weakened and she peered over her shoulder at the boys. *Who's in there?* Staring at the apartment window for a moment, she grabbed her cell phone and called Brian.

"I'm on my way. Don't move."

Hanging up with Brian, she tried to see into the window but couldn't see anyone. Twenty minutes later, after she had phoned the police, Brian showed up. He parked beside her car and left it running, Lucy in the backseat. Getting out of her car, Courtney met him underneath the covering that shielded the walkways to the apartment doors.

"Any idea who it might be?" His eyes stayed fixed on the window with the curtains closed.

"Nope."

"Did you call the police?"

"Yes. They said they'll send someone over shortly. That was five minutes ago." Coming closer to Brian, she grabbed hold of his arm. He wrapped an arm around her.

"It's going to be okay. Let me see if I can spot someone through the curtain." Letting her go, he walked over to the snow-covered flower bed and peeked into the window. He turned toward her. "It's a skinny blonde lady."

"What?" Sticking her head out, Courtney went over to his

side and peeked into the window. She saw Taylor in the kitchen. "That's my sister! What is she doing here?"

She pulled out her cell phone and called the police to tell them to cancel the car. After she hung up, she apologized as she rubbed her forehead.

"I'm sorry. I tried to see in there earlier and couldn't see anyone. Sorry for making you come over here."

He shook his head. "It's no problem. I'm glad you called. Let me help you get the boys inside."

Brian took Blaze while Courtney grabbed Todd, and they all four went into the apartment together. Brian left a few moments after Courtney introduced him to Taylor.

"How's Momma's boys doing?" Her arms were wide open and inviting as she sat on the couch with the two of them. Blaze and Todd were showing her random things like their cars and books.

"I love you, Tay!" Blaze randomly shouted.

"Mom. Not Tay." Her eyes went to Courtney, who was standing nearby. "Why are they calling me my nickname?"

"They just hear your nickname. I don't know. I try to correct them when I hear it."

Taylor spent the next two hours with the boys and then took them into the spare room and turned on a movie. When Courtney heard the television turn on, her heart dropped. Unable to stand by and let all the work she had done become unraveled, she went into the room and shut off the television.

"We don't watch TV to go to sleep anymore."

Rising from Todd's bed, Taylor came closer and lowered her voice. "Well, that's how *I* do it. They are *my* boys."

Smiling, Courtney nodded. "Yes, but they're able to fall asleep much sooner without TV. I highly recommend that you leave it off."

"Okay." Taylor dropped her hands. "No TV."

Taylor kissed the boys and came out into the living room with Courtney. Sitting down on the couch with Courtney, she finally explained what was going on.

"The rehab facility I was at shut down. I was doing so well that they said I could go home early and not have to transfer, so here I am."

Smiling, Courtney nodded as her mind raced. "Okay. So, what's the plan now?"

"I'm going to stay here, if that's okay, and get a job, then once I get money I'll move out."

"All right. Sounds great!" Hugging Taylor, Courtney was thrilled to see her sister looking healthy and heading in the right direction.

As she pillowed her head that night and prayed, she asked God to help her sister in recovery. As her thoughts and prayers drifted to Blaze and to Todd, Courtney's heart began to ache. "Lord? Help this pain in my heart and the worry plaguing my thoughts to go away. Let me trust in You alone. Whatever goes on with these boys will go on no matter what. Worry will not change that. Let my heart hold onto that reality. Amen."

CHAPTER 6

*O*n the following Sunday, Courtney went to church with Taylor and the boys. As they walked into the sanctuary, all of Courtney's friends from her ladies' group were complimenting her on how cute her boys looked in their Sunday school class. It was easy to notice her sister's disdain for the comments. When they finally took their seats, Taylor turned to Courtney.

"You just pretended like they were your kids?"

"No. Everybody knows they aren't mine. They just call them *my boys* because they've been coming for weeks now with me every Sunday." Leaning over, Courtney touched Taylor's arm. "Don't worry about it, Sis. I know it's hard. It's hard for me too."

Pastor Matt took to the stage and preached on the power of forgiveness. Though Courtney didn't reveal it to her, she knew she had to forgive Taylor for what she had done to the boys in the years prior to coming to live with her. She had, at the very least, neglected those boys in far more ways than she'd probably ever realize in this lifetime. Letting go of that bitterness and hurt inside her heart would be no easy feat, and Courtney knew it'd only be by the power of God that she'd ever let go.

"How'd you like the sermon?" Courtney's question came as they stood in line to pick up the boys.

"It was great. I was just thinking about forgiveness last night. You know, with Drake."

Courtney's heart dipped into her stomach. She shook her head. "You mean like, 'I forgive you, but I can't see you'?"

"No, I mean real God-honoring forgiveness. Get back with him. He told me last night on the phone that he has been sober for a week. I would've gone over there if he had the room for us."

Swallowing hard, it took everything inside of Courtney not to burst into tears or to slap her sister upside the head. "Oh, *Taylor . . .*"

Her sister responded sharply. "What?"

"Are you really thinking about going back to him? After everything?"

"Forgiving is the right thing to do." Taylor shook her head with a laugh in her tone. "Did *you* listen to the sermon?"

Tears welled in Courtney's eyes and she turned to hide them. Taylor grabbed her shoulder. "You're crying? What on earth for?"

Shaking her head, Courtney's heart broke apart in the moment. "Why would you go back to him? He was abusive and is a drug addict!"

"I love him, and that's the old him, Sis. You have to believe that I know what I'm doing." Folding her arms, Taylor didn't look at her again the rest of the time in line to get the boys.

After they got home, the two of them fed the boys and put them down for a nap. As Taylor and Courtney walked out of the spare room, Taylor stopped her in the hallway.

"Even though I don't want to, I'm going to be careful reintroducing the boys to Drake. I'm going to Drake's to hang out for a little bit. Is *that* okay with *you?*"

Relief filled Courtney knowing the boys wouldn't be going. "Yes. That's fine and a good idea not to take the boys."

Taylor still seemed upset toward her, but Courtney didn't care. The boys were the innocent ones in all of this, and they were safe, at least for now.

Right after Taylor left out the door, Courtney called her mother.

"Maybe you can talk to her, Courtney?"

"What?" Shaking her head, Courtney stood from the couch. "*Mom*. She just got out of rehab and went right back to Drake. I don't think she's going to listen to logic and reason here."

"Well, there's not much you can do about that. They aren't *your* kids."

Turning, Courtney glanced at the bookcase in the living room and walked over to it. She pulled out the copy of the signed document granting her temporary guardianship for six months. "She did sign guardianship over to me . . ."

"That was for during rehab and so you could take the children to the doctor! That wasn't so you could mess your sister's life up!"

Pushing the guardianship paper back into its place between two books on the shelf, she walked away. "I know, but those boys will not be going back to Drake's house. I guarantee that, Mom."

"You can't stop her, dear. No matter how hard you fight it."

Her mother's resistance left Courtney feeling agitated and alone. "I have to go."

Hanging up with her mother, she thought about calling Brian but decided against it. She didn't want to bother him with drama. Tossing her cell phone on the couch, she went down the hall and into her bedroom. Shutting the door, she got down on her knees and prayed.

"God." She paused, memories over the last couple months with the boys filling her thoughts. The progress she had made in their eating, sleeping, and structure. Hot tears burned in her eyes. "God, these boys are precious, and they deserve a loving home. I'm no better of a parent than anyone else, but I know those precious angels will be in danger at Drake's apartment." As her pulse ticked up, her prayer became more desperate. Folding her eyes into the bed, she rested her hands behind her head. "Lord, help me know Your will in all of this! Help me to see and help me to understand . . ."

That evening at seven o'clock when it was time to put the boys to bed, Courtney stared at the front door of her apartment. *Where are you, Taylor?* Sighing, she stood and went through all the same nightly rituals she had been doing for two and a half months with the boys, brushing teeth, prayers, and tucking them into bed. As she shut the door of their bedroom, she returned to the living room and checked her phone again. Her sister *still* hadn't called back or texted her a reply. It had now been six hours since she had gone over to Drake's apartment.

Tapping into her call log, she tried Taylor once more.

"This is me, leave a message!" *Beep!*

"Please call me. I'm worried . . ."

Hanging up, she sighed deeply. She thought about calling her mother but knew it wouldn't be of any use. Just then, Brian texted her.

Brian: Hey. How's everything going? You didn't seem your usual self at church. You okay?

Sniffling as his text brought a warm feeling of love over her, she smiled and opened the text on her phone.

Courtney: You saw that? Guess I'm not a very good actress.

My sister went back to her abusive boyfriend and hasn't called all day . . .

Her phone rang. It was Brian.

"Hello?"

"Hey. Where are the boys?" His tone was laced with worry.

"They're safe with me."

He sighed. "Thank goodness."

Courtney smiled. "You really do care, don't you?"

"Of course I do. So, how long has she been gone?"

"Six hours . . ."

"Yikes. No contact?"

"Nope."

"Was this boyfriend a drug addict too?"

"Yes."

"Man alive! Why do these women have to get caught up with such lousy men?"

"I don't know . . ."

"Can I come over?"

"If you want to. I'm just sitting here. Not a lot going on."

"You sound sad and I want to be there for you."

Wiping a tear, she smiled. "Okay. Thank you."

Hanging up with Brian, she stood up and went into the bathroom to brush her teeth and check her hair and makeup. She decided to stay dressed down in her pajamas since it was already after seven and they were more comfortable. Returning to the living room, she found a movie on a streaming service and popped some popcorn in the microwave.

A light knock sounded on the front door as she carried the bowl of popcorn into the living room. Setting it down on the coffee table, she went over and answered it.

It was Brian.

She embraced him for a long hug. "Thanks for coming. I appreciate it."

"No problem."

They went into the living room and sat down on the couch. Raising an eyebrow, Brian dug a hand into the bowl of popcorn. "You made us a treat."

Smiling, she nodded.

"There's that smile."

"Do you need a water or anything?" She went to stand up.

He rose up and motioned his hands downward. "Let me get it. You're always getting me stuff. Do you want something to drink as well?"

She shrugged playfully. "I wouldn't mind some tea."

Brian went into the kitchen and started checking cupboards. After the fourth sound of a cupboard opening, she laughed and looked over into the kitchen. "Right of the sink, lower drawer."

"Ahh. Kettle in a drawer. That's what threw me off." Listening to the sound of the faucet turn on and him filling the kettle reminded her of a different time in her life. When Drew was still alive and he'd heat water in that same chicken-themed kettle for their cups of tea. He'd always ask how many lumps of sugar, even though she always had two.

"What time did Lucy end up going home today?"

"Right after dinner Melissa came and got her." Walking back into the living room, Brian sat down on the couch and turned toward her. "Melissa seemed upset about something, but she wouldn't say what it was that was troubling her."

"Your ex-wife?" Raising an eyebrow, Courtney was surprised to hear him mention her.

"Yes. I know it's weird, but it's like even though it's over and has been over for a long time, I still care about her as a person even though she's kind of terrible. You know?"

Blinking rapidly to shoo the tears from her eyes as she

thought of Drew, she nodded. "I have my own battle with that and Drew. He's been gone for four years, but a part of my heart stays his forever. Sorry. That's weird to say to someone I'm dating."

"No, it's fine and it makes sense. When God fuses two people together in marriage, it's like super glue on wood. Yes, it can be torn apart, but it's an ugly mess that in some ways never changes. No matter how it separated." Right then, Brian reached one of his hands over and touched the top of her hand gently. Then ever so lightly, he squeezed.

"I couldn't imagine the pain you went through in losing your spouse."

Courtney shrugged, her gaze staying locked on Brian's brown eyes. "Mine left instantly and by no will of his own. Your spouse betrayed you. I think yours would be so much harder. Willingly being left? *Ouch.*"

Brian's head dipped. "It was hard."

Reaching her hand over, she lifted his chin. "But God works all things together for good. Even if we don't see it right away. Right?"

"Amen."

He got up and went into the kitchen, and her own words lingered on her mind a little while longer. *All things together for good.* Peering toward her hallway the led down to the spare room, she thought about Todd and Blaze. She wondered, *What's Your plan with those boys, Lord?*

Courtney snuggled up in Brian's arms after he returned with their cups of tea and she hit *Play* on the remote. His arms around her were a place of warmth, a feeling of security, and they sent waves of comfort washing over her entire body. As the movie ended a couple of hours later and the credits began to roll, she turned her head to look up at him. He turned his head to look at her.

Lifting his hand to her cheek, he gently grazed it and

looked into her eyes. Then he leaned in, planting his lips against hers softly. Ecstasy coursed through her body, radiating from the center of her chest outward. Turning her body to kiss him further, he brought his other hand up and held her face as he kissed her deeper.

Then she stopped and smiled. "You should go. The boys get up at five. That only gives me six hours of sleep if I go to sleep right now."

He raised his eyebrows. "Wow. What time did you used to wake up?"

"Eight to be to work by nine."

Brian shook his head and stood up from the couch. Turning toward Courtney as she rose to her feet, he smiled. "You're an amazing woman, Courtney. You're so selfless, raising those boys on your own for the last two months and possibly ending up raising them to adulthood if their mother doesn't work out."

She shrugged one shoulder as she thought about her mom. "Wish my mother would get that memo."

"What do you mean?"

"I told her about Taylor going back to Drake, and I mentioned the guardianship I have for six months and she flipped."

Holding out his hands, Brian shrugged. "You have to protect them. Right?"

"Right. You get it."

Brian came closer to her and wrapped her in a hug. "It's going to be okay."

After a long moment, they released and he pecked her on the lips once more and then left the apartment.

THREE DAYS LATER, BRIAN WAS working in his office one

afternoon and felt the two o'clock slow-down fast approaching. Lifting his coffee mug, he peered inside to see it was empty and then went down the hall to the kitchen. Walking in, he saw Courtney sitting at the kitchen island, crying.

"Whoa. What's wrong?" Coming around the island, he set his coffee cup down and wrapped his arms around her as he came in close over one shoulder. "Talk to me."

"Remember how Taylor hasn't come around since Sunday?"

"*Yes . . .*"

"She's demanding her boys and she's at the house with the cops right now."

Jumping back, Brian shouted. "What is she thinking?"

"I don't think she is. She has to be back on drugs."

"What are you going to do?"

She shrugged, looking at Brian with her red, swollen eyes. "I don't know. I just got her text and came in here to sit and breathe outside of view of the boys."

Recalling the guardianship Courtney had mentioned, he shook Courtney's shoulder. "The guardianship!"

"I know, but then that's going to start a whole thing with my mom and my sister. It's going to be ugly and I don't want that."

Coming around to the other side of the island, Brian leaned across the counter and grabbed both of her hands in his hands. "You have to decide what is more important, the well-being of these boys and doing whatever you can to protect them or saving face with your family."

"I'm scared, Brian."

"I'm sure you are scared. It's a scary thing. Whatever you need, I'll do. Want me to go with you over there?"

She shook her head. "No, I don't want the boys to be traumatized. Can you watch them, and I'll go over there and show the police the papers?"

"Absolutely. Go."

She grabbed her purse and kissed the boys, and then Brian, and left. Walking into Courtney's office that doubled as their playroom, Brian sat down with Blaze and Todd.

"What's going on, gentlemen?"

Todd brought over a car and handed it to him. Smiling, Brian took the toy and glanced around the room. Seeing a binder on the bookcase, he grabbed it and made a ramp. Then he placed the car at the top. Tapping the butt of the car, he made it rush down the angled binder and the car zoomed across the hardwood floor. Todd's eyes grew into saucers as he dashed over to the car and repeated the action Brian had just done. Blaze soon joined in on the action. After minutes turned into an hour, the boys were losing interest in the binder so Brian stood and rose to his feet.

"I'll be right back."

Hurrying down the hallway, he went and grabbed an old moving box he had broken down and folded, tucking it behind the desk in the study off the foyer. Returning to the playroom a few moments later, he took Courtney's desk chair and flipped it on its side. Then, he laid the box across the chair and showed the boys the *new* ramp.

Clapping, Todd jumped up and down. "Awesome, Brian!"

Sitting back against the wall, Brian watched as the two boys zipped their cars down the cardboard box ramp. He smiled. Only having raised one girl, Brian had never enjoyed the experience of raising and playing with boys. He started to wonder what else he had in his boyhood reservoir of memories.

———

PRAYING ON THE WAY OVER to the apartment, Courtney ignored every phone call from her mother. She knew her mother's feelings on the matter and they had no bearing anymore on what she had to do. Pulling into the parking lot of the apartment complex, she saw the cop cars along with Taylor and Drake. Her heart sank.

Shutting her car off, her hands trembled as she undid the seat belt and got out. Peering up at the snow falling down atop her head, she lifted a final prayer. *God, protect my heart and help me just get through this right now.*

As she walked toward the apartment, her sister immediately started cursing when she realized the children were not with her.

"Ma'am." An officer greeted her. "I understand you have Miss Taylor Hinley's children in your possession. Where are the children now?"

More cursing ensued from Taylor, and Drake even threw words in this time. A different police officer tried to calm the two of them down.

"They're safe with a friend. Come inside and I'll show you the guardianship papers."

Her sister became unhinged and tried to follow the two of them.

Courtney's heart ached, but she felt the supernatural power of God with her in that moment. "I'd prefer that she not enter my apartment."

"That's fine, ma'am. It'll just be me."

The other officer blocked Taylor's way to the apartment. More words of pain sliced through the cold wintry air, filling the atmosphere with venom and hate. Walking in with the officer, she went over to the bookcase and with trembling hands grabbed the guardianship papers that Taylor had signed and the court had approved. The officer looked them over.

"You understand that these are just temporary."

"Yes. That was originally what it was for, so she could go

to rehab. That man she is with is a drug addict and is abusive. I can't let these boys go with her there."

"I understand." The police officer jotted down notes. "Can you go ahead and give me your full name and birthday, please?"

She gave him all the information he wanted and then answered all of his questions. Handing the papers back to Courtney, he stopped before leaving. Turning around, he smiled and nodded at the teary-eyed Courtney. "I know this has to be hard for you. If all you told me today is the truth, you're doing the right thing. Just make sure you get a court date before those papers expire in mid-January."

"Will do. Thank you, Officer."

"We'll make sure the two of them are gone before we leave."

He exited out the door, shutting the door behind him. Before the door latched, Courtney could hear her sister crying hysterically out in the parking lot. Hurrying over to the door, she locked the deadbolt and then went to her bedroom and picked up her Bible. Opening to her daily reading plan, she began in Philippians chapter 3. As she made her way into chapter four, her inner being was quieting and renewing through the washing of the Word over her heart. Then a passage crossed her eyes that caused her to stop.

I can do all things through him who gives me strength.
Philippians 4:13

Her eyes watered, and she nodded as she peered up at the ceiling. "Yes, Lord. I can do *all* things through You alone. Teach my heart not to fret. Help me not to worry. Let this all be a lesson not only in grace and mercy, but in love and patience and reliance more on You. You are the breath in my lungs and the strength I need for each new day. It's been true since day one when those boys came to live with me, and it is still true today, Lord. Thank You!"

Rising from her bed a half hour after the police left, she checked out the blinds to make sure Taylor and Drake were gone from the premises.

Exiting her apartment, she locked the door and headed back to Brian's house. Arriving in the foyer, she couldn't hear a sound in the house. Confusion filled her thoughts as she journeyed down to her office. Walking into the room, she found her office chair tipped over, cardboard boxes and cars sprawled out, but no children and no Brian.

Then, through the window overlooking the back yard, movement caught her eye in the low light of the back yard and underneath the light pole. Walking over to the windows, she peered out to see Brian and the boys building a large snow slide down the side of the slope in the yard. Smiling as she covered her mouth, Courtney's heart melted and her eyes watered. *He's perfect. He's just like you wanted, Drew . . .* she thought to herself with tears in her eyes.

CHAPTER 7

COURTNEY - AGE 28

*D*rew was invited to be a guest speaker at a pastor conference, and this time it'd be over in Boise, Idaho. It wouldn't have been a big deal, but he had to drive without her in the snow and ice. She wouldn't be accompanying him on this trip since she was staying with her mother in Idaho Falls to help out while her father started another round of chemo. Courtney and Drew had been fighting all evening the night prior to his leaving.

Following him into the bedroom, Courtney stood with her hand on her hip as he flung clothes into a suitcase.

"You're just shutting down on me, now? Is that it, Drew?"

He stopped and turned toward her. "I don't know what else to say. We can't afford for me to fly and I need to be there. Have a little faith in God that I'll be okay."

Courtney rushed over to him and shoved him lightly back onto his heels. "Don't question *my* faith in God! I love God, but I don't think it's smart to drive on snow and ice!"

"And somehow, this would be fine if you were to go with me?" He laughed and shook his head as he continued packing. "Literally makes zero sense."

She grabbed his arm, forcing him to look at her. "You and I both know you aren't the best of drivers. I don't want you driving in the snow and ice at night."

"I'll get an extra night at the hotel. It'll be fine, sheesh."

She folded her arms, halfway okay with the idea. "Okay."

The following day, she wrote him a note and sneaked it into his luggage when he was in the shower.

Praying for you. I love you to the moon and back, hubby!

♡ *Wifey*

Entering their en-suite bathroom, she knocked lightly on the door as she could see the faint outline of his body through the frosted glass. She made a whistling sound.

He laughed from the shower. "You're such a goof."

She laughed. "I'm heading out to go over to my parents'."

"All right. I love you."

"Love you! Call me when you get there safely."

Exiting the bathroom, she went out to her car in the driveway. Getting into her car, she backed out of the driveway and headed over to her parents' house.

Arriving inside the door, the quietness and dark, gloomy feeling of the living room made that uneasy feeling return to her stomach. She felt it every time she set foot into the house after her father was diagnosed with cancer a few months ago.

Setting her purse down on the chair, she wove through the living room and went down the hall to her parents' bedroom.

Pushing open the door, she saw her father, Frank, asleep on the bed, a western playing on the TV atop the dresser. Her mother was reading one of her historical romance novels. Upon entering the room, her mother immediately noticed and shooed her out as she tossed the book she was reading and came toward the door. Pushing her out into the hall, Rhonda quietly shut the bedroom door and turned toward Courtney.

"Your father is finally asleep. Let's not disturb him."

"Okay. Where do you want me to start?"

"You can start in the kitchen and just work your way through the house from there."

"Where's Taylor?"

"She and Ralph went to a movie. They seem to be pretty good together. He seems kind and loving toward her."

"Yeah, I like him. Hopefully, he pops the question soon, eh?"

Rhonda shrugged. "Hopefully!"

Courtney got busy cleaning the entire house. Her mother was resistant to Courtney coming over and helping at first, when chemo started a few months ago, but she gave up trying to stop her. Courtney wanted to help in whatever way she could, and this was the best way she knew how—cleaning. As she finished cleaning, she saw it was already nine o'clock on her cell phone. *That's strange. He should've gotten to his hotel by now.*

She called Drew's cell phone and it went to voicemail.

Her stomach somersaulted.

She dialed the hotel.

He hadn't checked in.

Courtney called his cell phone again—no answer.

An hour later, she received a phone call from an unknown Idaho number.

"What's wrong with him?"

"Hello, is this Mrs. McAdams, Drew McAdams's wife?"

"It is."

"This is nurse Holly at Boise Medical Center. Your husband has been in an accident."

TWO MONTHS LATER, WHEN COURTNEY had finally gotten around to going through his belongings in his office, she found a sealed envelope addressed to her. On the back it read, **Only read if I'm dead ~Drew**

Morbid, she thought as confusion clouded her thoughts and she quickly opened the envelope. Unfolding the letter with trembling fingers, she began to immediately cry.

Courtney,

If you are reading this letter, that most certainly means I have passed away and you made it to the point where you could open my desk. To think of you having to deal with the pain of losing me is almost too much for my heart to bear. While I don't have a desire to pass away, I can't help but know it is possible. Knowing that it is possible, I felt compelled to write you this letter. Let me start by saying that being able to love you was the greatest gift God ever gave me in this life. You have always been my better half, and I thank you for choosing me. Thank you for making me the luckiest man in the world and thank you for putting up with me all of these years. I am sorry I left you too soon. If you are still young when you read this and I hadn't just left it in my desk for decades, I pray that you will remarry. Courtney, you must share that wonderful heart of yours that loves without expecting anything in return. I have no desire in my heart for you to live miserably on this planet without ever loving again. I do have some requests for such a man, though. First, he must be a God-fearing man. I pray that even through my death, you still have God at the center. God is the most important thing. Secondly, he must have kindness and politeness be the cornerstone of who he is as a person. You deserve respect and a partner who is genuine. Thirdly, he must love others, including children, because I know you two will have them. I have a gut feeling that you will indeed be a mother. Whether it's biological or adopting, you are going to be a mother, Courtney. I know it. I hope I'm right there with you when it happens, but if not, please know in your heart that I am so happy for you. If you're much older when reading this and none of this interests you, my deepest apologies and I hope you get as many naps as you can with me not around to bother you! May God strengthen you in the days ahead and bless the way in which you go with your life.

Sincerely yours,

Drew

Wiping tears from her eyes, she carefully folded the letter and slipped it back into the envelope. *Remarry?* She thought with pain and disgust. *Never shall I love another man as I have loved you, Drew McAdams. Never.*

After her father passed away six months after Drew, her mother gave her and Taylor each ten thousand dollars from the life insurance policy to move out of the house and find their own way in life. Rhonda was selling the house and moving to a one-bedroom studio to *live alone in misery the rest of my years on the planet,* her own words, not anyone else's. Courtney tried to stay near, but her mother insisted that she start over somewhere.

With her ten thousand, Taylor decided to party until it

was gone. She used the cash to finance a numbness that would last for months.

Courtney, on the other hand, decided to move away from Blackfoot and live in Eastern Washington, more specifically, Spokane, Washington, where Drew was originally born. She found a cute little two-bedroom apartment and kept most of her money from the life insurance policy in savings while she worked and figured out what she was going to do with the rest of her life. She wasn't sure exactly what she wanted to do, but she realized it wasn't to stay in Blackfoot with her bitter mother and sister who was heading down a path of darkness.

Taylor showed up on Courtney's doorstep in Spokane one snowy night, near the one-year anniversary of when Drew had passed away. It had only been six months since their father had died.

"What are you doing in Spokane?"

Rubbing her belly, she shook her head and started to cry as her breath was visible in the cold night air. "I need to go to rehab, Sis. I have a little bean inside me. I need a place to crash tonight, then I go in the morning to a rehab out in Mead, just outside of town."

"Wow. Yeah, come on in and crash here." Stepping aside, she let Taylor into her apartment.

After heading to bed that night, Courtney lay beneath the covers and cried herself to sleep. Here her sister was with a kid on the way and unmarried. Rolling onto her back in bed, Courtney peered up at the dark ceiling. Her heart was aching after yesterday's trip down Memory Lane with Drew. She spent the whole day crying, but the worst part was that nobody reached out to her. It felt like a prison of isolation, and nobody cared how she felt. "I know You care for me, Lord. It's just hard to feel Your love right now. It feels so far away from my heart. Teach my aching heart to sense when You are near."

Leaning over, she turned on the light and pulled out the envelope with Drew's letter in it from the nightstand beside the bed. She wept as she read the words over again and Drew's requirements of the perfect man for her. *It'll never happen. Not in a million years will I give my heart away again.*

CHAPTER 8

*B*uckling the boys into their car seats that following Thursday evening, Courtney got into the car and headed over to Susan's house for her ladies' Bible study a little earlier than normal. She wanted to tell April, one of the women she had become close friends with, about what had happened with her sister, Taylor. Parking in the driveway at Susan's house, she went inside, and April's daughter, Kimberly, took the boys to go play. Courtney entered the kitchen where April and Susan were preparing snacks.

Sitting down on a stool at the island beside April, she turned toward her.

"She tried to come back and get them."

April set the knife down she was using to cut cubes of cheese and turned toward her. "*No.*"

"Yes. It was terrible. She was cursing and screaming and crying. There were cops and everything."

"What'd you do?"

"Showed the police the guardianship papers."

"How'd the boys react?"

Susan walked over to the island, concern apparent on her face as she listened to their exchange.

"They didn't have to see any of it. I left them with Brian and went to handle it."

"Your boss?" April stuck out her neck.

"*Well . . .* he's more than just my boss now. We've kind of started seeing each other."

Susan smiled and leaned against the island's top. "Brian is a great guy. It's a shame what Melissa did to the poor man. She worked a real number on him and broke him to pieces. I didn't think he'd ever enter the relationship arena again."

Courtney raised her eyebrows. "Why did you think that?"

Susan laughed and stood upright. "Because he announced to everyone that he was done with relationships after everything happened."

"Oh. Well, everything seems to be going okay." Turning to April, then to Susan, Courtney's eyes watered as she thought of the boys. "I'm just worried about the boys."

April placed a hand on Courtney's back. "It's going to be okay. They are safe with you."

"Yeah, until next month." Tears spilled over and onto her cheeks. She wiped them as she shook her head. "I have a court date January second for permanent guardianship, but she's going to protest it."

"Do you have a lawyer?"

Sniffling, she shook her head. "It's not that kind of thing. You don't have personal lawyers present for it. It'll just be me, her, the judge, and a CPS lawyer guy."

"You think she'll win?"

Thinking of how the kids used to stay at Drake's apartment, she nodded. "I'm worried she will win. I just want those boys to have healthy and good lives, and being with drug addicts and abuse in the home isn't how that happens. You know?"

"You can tell the judge that, right?" April inquired.

"It's just hearsay unless there is proof." Raking her hands through her hair, she rested her elbows on the island as she looked downward. "I don't know what to do."

"Pray and trust God." April picked her knife back up and continued cutting cubes of cheese for the snack platter. "I know it seems generic, but I'm telling you. When Justin and I went through a rough patch, I was a wreck. Ask Susan."

She lifted her eyes to Susan, and Susan nodded lightly. "And so was I when I lost my husband. What I've learned over the years is that life isn't always pretty, but God *is* always working. I know it's hard to see it, but you will see it."

Courtney's heart was starting to feel a measure better. "Thank you, Ladies."

"Now, tell us more about you and Brian." April raised an eyebrow. "When did that happen?"

A light laugh lifted from Courtney's lips as she smiled and shook her head. "It just kind of happened. You know? I mean, I've been attracted to him since the day I first met him. When I dropped the boys off in Sunday school class for the first time, I saw him standing in the classroom serving children cereal. I was a hot mess, but I noticed how well put together he was. Then he hired me, and I started working for him, and one thing led to another."

"Wow. Well, I hope it works out." April scooped up the cubes of cheese and set them on the platter. "We have a special guest speaker tonight. It's a pastor's wife from Diamond Lake."

"Oh, wow. Really?" Courtney perked up at hearing it. "What is she speaking on?"

"She'll be talking about forgiveness. Susan enjoyed Pastor

Matt's sermon so much on the topic back when he preached on it that she wanted to have someone come and speak on it."

That evening, as all fifteen of the women in attendance sat on couches, chairs, and the floor, Susan led a prayer and then the guest speaker took to the floor.

"Good evening, all. My name is Serenah, and today, I want to speak to you about forgiveness. It's a hard topic for me, personally, because there've been a few people in my life that I had to forgive. One in particular, who was most difficult, was my first husband, who abused me."

The room was quiet as she surveyed the ladies in the circle.

"You probably think it was just the physical side of abuse, his hitting me, but that was only partially what I had to forgive him for. The biggest part and the most painful part was losing my child while I was still pregnant."

Courtney's eyes widened, eager for her to continue.

"You see, I had run away from him and that marriage to protect myself and the baby I was carrying, but . . . I ended up miscarrying anyway. I blamed him for it. For years, I tucked away the pain of it, and then one day, I heard a story. This missionary and his wife had gone overseas to an Islamic terrorist war-torn country to serve. One day, while his wife was working at the local hospital and he was off helping some locals, she was gunned down by terrorists. He didn't know about it until he went over to the hospital and found her lying in a pool of her own blood. He fell prostrate on the floor and thanked God for the time he had with her while she was on this earth. Then, years later, he remarried and went on another missionary trip to that same country and preached in that exact spot where he had found her. What did he preach on? The power of forgiveness."

Whispers around the room filled the atmosphere. "Wow" and "How is that possible?"

Serenah stopped walking and looked around at the women. "The point of this is to say the devil wants to disable, disarm, and immobilize his people any way he can. He already knows he has lost the fight with those who claim the name of Jesus. So what's the next-best thing for him? To keep them ineffective and not producing fruits of the Spirit in their lives." Walking over to a chair with papers on it, she picked up the pile of worksheets and began to hand them out. "This is a worksheet to help you understand the pain spots in your heart and to identify where forgiveness is needed. Maybe there's a sibling or relative you have been giving a 'good letting alone,' as my late grandmother, Emma, would say. Maybe it's more subtle. A parent you feel hurt by daily. We all have people in our lives we need to forgive because we all are sinners. The question is, are we actively forgiving? Or are we holding on and letting the root of bitterness grow?"

As Serenah handed Courtney her paper, she knew exactly the two names she needed to write. First, Taylor, and secondly, her mother, Rhonda.

"We don't forgive other people because they came and apologized to us or they 'made things right.' No, Biblical forgiveness doesn't operate that way. Biblical forgiveness is between you and God, primarily, not just you and others. Turn in your Bibles to Colossians 3."

Courtney picked her Bible up from the side of her chair and flipped to the book and chapter. Then, Serenah read verse thirteen.

Bear with each other and forgive one another if any of you has a grievance against someone. Forgive as the Lord forgave you.
Colossians 3:13

"Our sins and our wrongs have been forgiven by God. When we repent and confess our wrongdoings, He is mighty to forgive *always*. In turn, we have no right to hold back on forgiveness toward the people in our lives. No matter the pain they have caused. Even if they gun your wife down in a hospital or . . ." —her hand found her stomach— "take away someone's future."

A hand went up and Serenah called on the lady.

"But doesn't it just allow the person to keep hurting us? How is that what God wants?"

"Sometimes, a person can still hurt us if we let them back into our lives. I'm glad you brought that up. Listen, Ladies. You can forgive without giving trust. You can love without being accepting of bad behavior. These are common misconceptions that we all have. Forgiveness is releasing the debt someone owes you, nothing more than that."

Melody, one of the ladies in the group with tears in her eyes, raised a hand.

Serenah nodded to her. "Go ahead."

Wiping the tears from her eyes, she stammered as she tried to speak. "A few months ago, my daughter was killed in a car wreck by a drunk driver. I . . ." She started crying, and Serenah came over to her and bent her knees, wrapping an arm around her. Courtney's heart sank as Melody continued. "I am trying so hard to forgive the man who did it, but it just feels impossible."

"I couldn't imagine that." Serenah's cheeks moistened with tears. "That has to be the most difficult thing for a parent to ever endure. I'm so sorry."

As the night went on, Courtney realized just how much unforgiveness she had been harboring toward her sister and mother. Lifting a prayer of thankfulness to God for all the protection He had provided her and her family with, she realized she needed a more thankful heart. On her way out to the car that evening with the boys, Courtney felt determined to focus on the love of God every time a moment of bitterness rose within her. If someone like Melody, who lost their child in a car wreck, could be striving toward forgiveness and love toward the perpetrator, she could too. *With You, God, all things are possible.*

THE NEXT MORNING, BRIAN SPOTTED Courtney pulling into the roundabout from inside his truck. He turned toward Lucy, who was sitting in the passenger seat, staring out at the frozen fountain just outside her window.

"Hey. I'll be right back and then we can go."

"*Okay.*"

He got out of the truck and walked through the snow toward Courtney's car. He made his way over to the driver's side window. She rolled the window down and peered up at him.

"What's this surprise, Brian?"

"You'll have to follow me and see." He smiled and then peered into the backseat and saw Blaze and Todd bundled up just as he had instructed her in the text message that morning. The boys looked like little black marshmallows in their car seats.

Traversing the driveway back to his truck, he got in and shut the door of the pickup. Taking off his snow gloves, he rubbed his hands together and then turned the key over as he pumped the gas. His old Chevy pickup truck could've easily been replaced since *Puppy Chow Direct* took off, but it was a gift from his late father and an item he'd never part with as long as he was alive and it was functional.

"Why can't you tell me where we're going, Dad?" Lucy inquired as she pulled her scarf down from her lips. "I'm not a little kid."

"It's called a surprise for a reason, Princess, and yes, you're still a child."

She peered through the back window of the truck and then over at her dad. "We're going to that Christmas tree lot over off Sullivan street, aren't we?"

He shrugged and shifted the truck into gear. Driving around the roundabout, he glanced over at his daughter with a smile. "I guess you'll have to wait and see."

When the city landscape turned to country fields and snow-topped trees, Lucy again turned to Brian. "Wait. Where are we going? We're leaving Spokane?"

"What do you want for Christmas this year?"

"You haven't gotten anything for me yet?" Lucy leaned toward him, her eyes wide. "It's next week, Dad!"

"I know. That's why I need to know what you want. I tried doing some browsing online the other day, and I couldn't figure out if you'd want a toy of some kind or an older kid thing. You're at a strange age."

"Okay." Tapping her chin for a moment, she then turned toward him. "I know! I saw this cool nail thing you just shove your fingernail in and it paints it. How about that?"

"I'll keep that in mind. What about baby dolls? You always love getting one of those."

"Oh, yes, of course, a baby doll and a highchair too."

Smiling as he took an exit off the freeway, his heart warmed. She might've been getting older, but she was still his little girl. If he could just hold onto the child-like wonder and excitement she still had, maybe she'd skip the teenager years and stay sweet as an apple.

"Okay. This is weird, Dad." Adjusting in her seat, Lucy's eyes were glued out her window as they took another turn and were suddenly on a country road out in Chattaroy. She turned toward him. "I don't get how there is anything out here for us all to do."

He didn't respond. Slowing the truck down, he pulled off the road into a turnaround spot off the road and parked. Courtney parked her car and started to get the boys out of the back. Getting out of the truck, he went to the bed of the truck and retrieved his axe.

Lucy's gaze caught the sight of the axe. "We're going to cut down a Christmas tree!"

Courtney smiled at Brian as they all met between the vehicles near the fence line.

Pointing the axe toward the spotty field of trees planted in every direction, Brian nodded. "Let's go find *our* Christmas tree."

They all traversed the two feet of snow in search of the perfect tree.

Blaze started to get fussy and Brian took notice. Stopping, he bent a knee and peered into the little man's eyes. "What should we name the tree?"

"Steve."

Brian let out a hearty laugh and stood up. "Steve. I like it!" Turning his gaze toward a nearby tree, he started leading them over to it.

"Doesn't look like a Steve to me." Courtney's comment lifted as she inspected the tree. "Looks more like a Tony."

Brian let out a laugh. "Let's keep looking."

They continued through the snow. Brian's face was starting to feel the cold wintry bite of December set into his cheeks as a breeze blew in. Arriving at a nice six-footer without a weird deformity, he patted it and turned toward Courtney and the children.

"Is this one *Steve?*"

Blaze did a thumbs-up with his gloves while he ate a handful of snow. The other kids and Courtney nodded.

Lucy spoke up. "Any tree will do at this point. I'm cold and want to leave, Dad."

Smiling, he pointed behind him. "Everyone stand back while I cut it down."

Swinging his axe, Brian connected with the cold tree, cutting at an angle and sending bark flying. He hit a few more times until it fell. Dragging it across the snow, they all journeyed through the field back toward their vehicles. The boys and Lucy were behind him and Courtney. Coming closer to him, Courtney wrapped her arm through his, sending a warmth through him that thawed a part of the invading winter cold.

At the truck, he hoisted the whole tree into the bed and then shut the gate.

After securing the tree with straps, he climbed into the driver seat of the truck. Lucy appeared upset. Her arms were crossed and her cheeks moist with tears.

"What's wrong?"

She shook her head and looked out her window as he turned the key over and pulled the truck out onto the road. Replaying the events that had transpired, Brian was at a loss as to what had happened.

"I honestly don't know what I did to upset you, but I'm sorry."

"She's not *Mom.*"

The three words were colder than the ice stuck to the rims of his truck. He realized they had walked closely together on the way back with the tree. His heart broke for his daughter as he looked again at her disappointed expression and her tears streaming down her cheeks.

"I know she's not your mother, Princess. She will never be your mother."

"Then why do I get the feeling that you like her?"

He hesitated for a moment to have the conversation but decided she was old enough to hear it. "Well, I do like her. She's a nice lady with a kind heart, and I can't help but enjoy having her around."

Sniffling mingled with his daughter's silence in the following few moments.

"Listen, I know this kind of thing must be hard for you. I get that, and I'm here to talk about it whenever you need to chat. I love you."

"I just feel like you have this whole life outside of me."

"That's not true. You are very much a part of my life."

"Sure, when I come over one weekend a month."

"That's something you have to talk to your mother about if you are unhappy with it. You can spend more time with me, if you'd prefer. Personally, I'd like to have you every weekend."

"But then I miss out on my other family over at Mom's house." Lucy rested her head against her hand. "It's not fair. No matter what, I lose. Either I'm missing out on stuff over there or over here with you. I feel stuck and I hate it."

Pulling over to the side of the road, Brian went to Courtney's car as she slowed and told her to head back to the house and that he'd catch up with her soon. Then he went over to the side of the truck where Lucy was sitting. Opening her truck door, he peered into her eyes and grabbed both of her hands gently.

"Look at me, my daughter."

She lifted her swollen and puffy eyes to her father.

"I love you, and I know it sucks how things have to be in your life with two different homes. It's super lame, and I *never* wanted this life for you, but it's the cards you were dealt, dear. I'm not saying it's okay the way it is, but I am telling you right now that it's going to be as okay as you allow it to be. And just so you know, for me, it's been the most difficult things in my life that taught me the most about God's love for me. Let Him show His heart to you, my child."

She rolled her eyes and looked away.

"Hey. Don't be disrespectful because you're hurting inside. Come here and give me a hug."

They hugged for a long moment. As they did, Brian prayed over and for his daughter. *Help her, Lord. Strengthen her heart and help her see Your love and experience it for herself. Amen.*

As they released, Brian raised his eyebrows.

"Listen. Do you want to go see the warehouse where all the puppy food is made?"

Her eyes lit up and she nodded excitedly. Brian had been promising for months to take her, but he hadn't found the time to do it.

"Okay." He was about to shut the door when he paused and looked at her again. "Life gets harder the older you get, kid, but having a relationship with God is what helps you get through it."

She nodded and sat up a little straighter in her seat.

Walking around to his side of the truck, he got in and called Courtney, letting her know they'd be an hour or so.

WARMING APPLE CIDER ON THE stove in the kitchen, Courtney went into the living room to check on the boys. They had the ornaments out of the boxes and were throwing them at each other. Rushing over to the two of them, she scooped them both up into her arms. Setting Blaze on one couch, she took Todd over to another and sat him down. Lowering to her knees, she peered into his eyes.

"Todd. You know we aren't supposed to touch those until Brian and Lucy get back."

He pointed to Blaze. "He did it."

Grabbing his hand, she flipped it over to reveal the sparkles that had fallen from the ornament onto his hand. "Don't lie, Todd."

His head dipped. "I'm sorry, Mom."

Neither of the boys had called her that in over a week. Hearing the name caused her heart to jerk as she thought about the coming court date. Rising, she took him gently by the hand, along with his brother, and led them down to the playroom where there was less for the two of them to get into.

Coming back to the kitchen, she was surprised to see Brian standing over the pot of apple cider, stealing a drink from the ladle.

"Caught you."

He laughed and set the ladle on the counter. "It smelled too good in here not to snag a drink."

Peering around, Courtney raised an eyebrow. "Where's Lucy?"

"She's grabbing a saw from the garage and is going to attempt to cut the end of the tree for us." Brian walked over to Courtney in the kitchen and pulled her in close to him. Smoothing her hair back behind her ear, he grazed her cheek with the warmth of his palm. "I figured I could sneak in here and steal a kiss."

Her heart melted as he leaned in to kiss her. His movements were slow and purposeful. It was as if he did everything on purpose and nothing by chance, calculated and well thought out.

His lips pressed against hers and heat traveled down her

body. His embrace, his kiss, his everything were exactly what she wanted, exactly what she needed.

Separating a moment later, he smiled and nodded. "There, I'm all good now. I'll be back in soon with the tree and Lucy."

He was about to leave, but she stopped. "Wait. Is everything okay with Lucy?"

Brian stopped and turned toward her. Nodding, he glanced at the kitchen floor then lifted his gaze to Courtney. "She's okay. Just struggling a little bit with me and you."

Courtney remembered Lucy's comments in the hallway when they first met. Lifting a hand to shield her mouth, she looked at Brian. "Is it my fault? I remember telling her I was just an employee. I didn't—"

He held a hand up. "It's all right. I got it handled. She's just getting older and to that age where girls and guys have a bit of an identity crisis. Toss in the fact that she has two different homes . . ." He shrugged. "It's tough."

"I bet." Courtney came closer to him, feeling drawn to his concern over his daughter. Touching his chest gently, she looked him in the eyes. "You're a good dad, Brian."

A light sarcastic laugh lifted from his lips. "It's hard to know that sometimes."

"You are."

"You're a good Mom too."

He turned and left to go back outside and help Lucy. His words lingered over her heart and in her thoughts. *Good Mom.* The reality was that she wasn't a mother at all. She had merely taken care of her sister's children, and soon, that could all be changing.

After hanging the ornaments all together, the three children sat down on the couch with Courtney while Brian told them a story out of the Bible.

" 'Then the Lord shut him in.' When you first read the

story of Noah, at least for me, I didn't think anything about this verse. Can any of you tell me something interesting about Genesis 7:16? I'll read it again."

The animals going in were male and female of every living thing, as God had commanded Noah. Then the Lord shut him in.
Genesis 7:16

Lucy raised a hand and Brian called on her. "Every animal had a male and female?"

"That's true, but there's something else. Courtney, you want to take a shot?" His eyes shifted to her and her pulse ticked up as his warm brown eyes focused on her.

"God shut the door?"

"Yes. Exactly. *God* shut the door. Imagine the door for the ark. How massive it had to be."

Blaze was chewing on his shirt and Todd was staring at the tree lights, neither paying attention.

Courtney tapped each of their legs.

"Boys, pay attention."

Brian continued, "What's fascinating is the fact that Noah had to have built a door that he couldn't alone close. That takes some pretty amazing faith, right?"

Lucy nodded, and the boys were still unable to listen, but Brian kept his cool.

"Todd." Brian captured his attention. "Try to lift that couch over there."

Smiling, he scurried over to the nearby empty couch and attempted to lift it. He grunted and tried three times. Blaze went over and tried too, but it was of no use.

Laughing, Brian directed them back to the other couch.

"It's heavy, huh, boys?"

The boys nodded.

"Noah made a giant door he knew only *God* could close. He had faith and trust in God that He would close the door when the time was right. Let's go ahead and pray."

Bowing their heads, Brian led a closing prayer. After the prayer was over, Lucy took the boys outside to play in the snow while Courtney stayed inside with Brian in the living room. Courtney grabbed the stereo remote and turned on light Christmas music. They sat together looking at the tree covered in lights and ornaments. Courtney moved in closer to Brian on the couch and snuggled up to him.

"Taking the day off today was a great idea. It's been really fun."

"I agree." Resting his arm around her a little more, Brian surveyed the tree in its entirety. "There's a lot to be thankful for this Christmas season. Having you and the boys come into my life has been wonderful."

"Same." Lifting herself away from his embrace, she turned toward him as she recalled last night's teaching on forgiveness. "Have you forgiven Melissa?"

"Whoa. What?"

Courtney smiled, sensing his confusion of the topic coming out of nowhere. "I'm just thinking of last night's Bible study. We had a guest speaker who spoke about forgiveness."

"Ah, over at Susan's place. Hmm, I think I have forgiven her."

"That's good. I realized through last night that I need to work on forgiving my mother and sister. Especially my sister. I hold what she has done against her, and I need to let that go."

"Yep. Because of the forgiveness that Christ has extended to us."

"Exactly." Courtney smiled warmly, glad to hear he understood the connection of forgiveness to the Gospel. "I just don't know how that forgiveness looks in real-to-life application. You know? Is it, 'Here's your kids, have a great life?' "

"No, not at all." He sat up and turned his body toward Courtney. "That's putting the children in danger. Forgiveness isn't passivity. It's releasing that person of the debt."

He paused, appearing as if a light bulb went off in his head.

"What is it, Brian?"

His gaze turned toward the large windows overlooking the back yard where Lucy and the boys were playing. He stood up. "Maybe I haven't totally forgiven Melissa."

Courtney stood and walked over to the window with him. She peered over at Brian. "What do you mean?"

"Earlier today, while I was walking around with Lucy at the warehouse and showing her all around, I kept thinking about how it was all Melissa's fault. She was the one who cheated. She was the one who tore this family apart at the seams."

"And you thought you had forgiven her?"

He turned toward Courtney. "Yes. I don't hate her. I just don't like her. I accept that she's with Conrad . . . kind of . . . and I don't want to see her die or anything. I also have moved on in my heart. I like you. But what I'm starting to realize is I haven't released her of that debt at the heart level. You know? I feel as if she owes me for what she has done. That's without even mentioning that the worst result of all from what she has done still exists." He stopped short, appearing uneasy about continuing.

"What is it, Brian?" She came closer, touching his chest.

"I'm scared of losing you like I lost her."

"I'm not going anywhere."

"Yeah." His eyes went to the kids in the yard playing in the snow. "She wasn't, either."

"That's not fair to me."

"I know." He turned toward her and took both of her hands in his. Bringing them up to his lips, he kissed the top of her hands. "It's not fair at all, and I'm fighting against that feeling inside. I'm learning to trust."

CHAPTER 9

On Christmas morning, at a quarter past five, Courtney was startled awake by the sound of a loud crash in the living room of her apartment. Leaping from the covers, she darted out from her bedroom and down the hallway.

Coming out into the living room, her heart dipped. The Christmas tree was lying on the floor, ornaments broken all over place and two smiling boys who had opened every present from under the tree.

"What did you boys do?" Courtney asked as tears filled her eyes. Walking through the carnage of wrapping paper, her heart was heavy. "I asked you not to open presents until I was awake."

"Why didn't I get a sword like Blaze?" Todd's question completely neglected the fact that she had uttered a word.

Staring up at the ceiling, Courtney prayed. *Lord, strengthen me. I need You.* Bringing her attention back to Todd and to Blaze, she lowered herself down to their eye level.

"It breaks my heart that you two disobeyed. Now, listen, you need to help me clean this up."

Todd threw himself onto the floor and started crying. Blaze ran away down the hallway and into the bedroom.

Picking up the tree, Courtney set it back into place and then threw away the broken ornaments and hung the non-busted ones back onto the tree. By that time, Todd had calmed down.

"Come here, Todd." Opening her arms, Courtney motioned for him to come in for a hug. He came in closer and wrapped his arms around her as he rested his swollen tear-filled eyes against her chest.

"I miss my mom."

Her heart ached and she rubbed his back. "I know you do, bud."

Peeling him off her, she looked him in the eyes. "Listen, do you think it was okay what you did? Opening all the presents when I was asleep?"

He dipped his chin and shook his head. "*No . . .*"

"That's right, it's not okay. What do you need to do about it?"

"Say sorry?"

"Remember what can we say instead of 'sorry'?"

"Will you forgive me?"

Courtney smiled and nodded. "Yes. I will forgive you. Can you help me clean up?"

"Yes."

Retrieving a garbage bag from the kitchen, she handed it to him and went down the hallway to retrieve Blaze from the bedroom. Walking into the bedroom, she saw Blaze playing with his little blocks, building a tower.

Sitting down next to Blaze, she watched him for a moment as he finished the last block on top of the tower. His eyes grew wide as he looked at the tower, then over to her.

"That's an awesome tower, Blaze. Good job."

He swung a fist and smashed the tower of blocks, sending them crashing to the floor.

Pulling him into her lap, she held him. "What did I say last night about the presents, Blaze?"

"No opening."

"That's right. So, what did you do this morning by opening them?"

"Disobeyed . . ." His little eyes fell to the floor, remorse evident in his posture. She placed a hand on his back.

"Is disobeying okay?"

"No. I'm sorry. Forgive me?"

"I forgive you. Go help your brother clean up and then we'll have breakfast."

"Okay!"

Jumping up, he ran down the hallway to go help his brother in the living room.

Standing up, she looked over at the desk. Walking over to it, she sat down in the chair and pulled out journals, searching for a Christmas entry. Finding one, she relaxed into the desk chair and read.

12/25/2010

Bible reading: 1 Thessalonians 4-5

Focus: 1 Thessalonians 5:16-18 states, 'Rejoice always, pray continually and give thanks in all circumstances; for this is God's will for you in Christ Jesus.' What a beautiful reminder of the will of God in my life.

Prayers:

Help my heart to be always rejoicing and thankful in all circumstances, Lord. I realized this morning after Courtney and I exchanged gifts and we were sipping on our morning tea that the gifts were nice, but the true and greatest gift was what You did on the Cross. What You did by taking on the form of a child. I've heard the Christmas story for years, but it wasn't until this year that I really meditated on the fact that You became a mere human being, and for what? For us. For me. You took the form of a human, Lord. Let my heart rejoice in that all the days of my life. Let me have a heart that is thankful for Your sacrifice which allows me the opportunity to be in a relationship with You, my Creator, my God.

Smiling, Courtney closed the journal and thought over her life and how much there was to be thankful about. She thought of Melody, the woman at the ladies' Bible study who had lost her daughter just a few months ago. She was waking up today for her first Christmas without her daughter. Courtney's heart ached for her.

Leaving the room, she went into her bedroom and grabbed her cell phone from the nightstand. She sent a text to Melody.

Courtney: Praying for you today.

Walking out into the living room, she saw the boys had managed to clean almost the entire floor of the wrapping paper.

"Good job, boys! I'm so proud of you. Let's get you some breakfast, then we'll video chat with Grandma."

"What about Brian?" Todd asked.

"We'll see him later this morning. It's Christmas, so we should let him sleep in."

As she prepared breakfast for the boys, eggs and toast, she lifted a rejoiceful prayer to Heaven. She had food to eat, children to love on, a boyfriend who was Godly, and a roof over her head.

THE DOORBELL CHIMES RANG AT nine o'clock and brought his

devotional time to an end. Closing his Bible, he set it on the coffee table and went into the foyer to answer the door.

"Merry Christmas!" Brian cheered as he opened his arms and bent down to embrace the boys. "Go look under the tree!"

They darted through the foyer to the living room.

He stood up and embraced Courtney in a hug. "Merry Christmas."

"Merry Christmas, Brian. I'm thankful for you."

As they released, he smiled. "I'm thankful for you as well. How'd the morning go with the boys?"

She smiled as they walked through the foyer. "Good. They got up pretty early."

He laughed. "I bet!"

Walking together into the living room, the boys were looking at the presents, looks of uncertainty on their faces.

Todd's eyes were glued to Courtney. "Can we open them?"

"Well, of course!" Brian came closer to the boys, who were each holding a gift in their hands. "Do you have the right ones?"

Peering at the name tags on the gifts, he nodded. "You managed to find the right ones. Go ahead."

"Good job waiting, boys." Turning to Brian, she explained the morning to him.

"Ahh, I see. It's good that they learned from it."

Brian and Courtney sat down on the couch. She turned toward him. "What time is Lucy coming over?"

"This afternoon. Hey, there's a New Year's Eve gathering at the warehouse. I was wondering if you wanted to go with me?"

Courtney peered over at the boys. "I don't know if I can find a sitter."

"Oh, I didn't mean just you. You can bring the boys with

you. It's for the employees and their families. We have fire-works and a big dinner. It's a lot of fun."

"All right. Yes, count us in!"

"Great. It'll be fun."

Todd ran over with his Nerf gun. "Can you open it for me?"

Receiving the package into his hands, Brian nodded and pulled out his pocketknife. Cutting the plastic, his eyes grew wide. "Whoa. This thing is awesome. Be careful and don't point it at anyone. Got it?"

Todd nodded excitedly as he took the gun back into his hands. He started loading nerf bullets into the chamber on the side.

Courtney watched as Todd loaded it. "These boys make everything into guns."

He laughed. "I know. I figured that's why Nerf guns would be fun for them. I wasn't a hundred percent sure you'd be okay with it . . . but I went with my gut."

Peering over at him, her glance and smile melted his heart. "It was a good idea. Thank you."

Todd lifted his gaze to Brian. "Thank you, Brian!"

"You're welcome, Champ."

"I almost forgot." Courtney grabbed her purse from beside the couch and pulled it onto her lap. Retrieving a small rectangular box from inside, she handed it to him.

Taking the small blue box with a ribbon into his hands, he shook his head. "You shouldn't have gotten me anything."

"I wanted to."

"I didn't get you anything."

"That's okay."

He laughed and looked over at the tree. "It's in the tree."

She tilted her head and raised her eyebrows. "Really?"

Rising, she went over to the tree and searched the

branches. Pulling a white box out, she came back over to the couch.

"You open your gift first."

She shook her head. "I gave you yours first. You open first."

"Okay, okay." Lifting the lid of the blue box, he found inside a digital smart watch that records his steps and workouts. "Wow. Thank you!"

"You're welcome." Unwrapping her white box, she stopped and covered her mouth. "Oh, Brian. It's beautiful."

"It's just a little something I picked up. When I saw it, I thought of you."

Pulling out the heart-shaped pendant on a white gold chain, her lips curled into a smile. "It's wonderful. Thank you. Can you help me put it on?"

"Yes."

Taking it into his hands, he unclasped the chain as she turned and lifted her hair up from her neck. Placing the necklace around her neck, he clasped the ends together.

Turning toward him, she touched the pendant.

"How's it look?"

Peering into her eyes, he smiled and leaned in. "It's perfect."

Then he kissed her.

THE FOLLOWING WEEK WAS NEW Year's Eve, and Courtney was nervous about making a good impression on Brian's employees and their families. She knew it'd be a great time, but she wasn't sure how the boys would do with the loud sounds of the fireworks. The blow dryer and vacuum were known to strike fear in their hearts, so she couldn't imagine what the sound of explosions would do.

Arriving just after six that evening, she was relieved to see children the boys' ages there, and they also had games and a jumpy castle set up for the children. Immediately, Todd and Blaze kicked their shoes off and ran for the castle.

Spotting Brian in a group of people chatting, Courtney went and found a seat at an open table. Sitting down, she set her purse under her chair and then went and grabbed plates of food for the boys.

As she made her way through the line of food, she held a plate in each hand for the kids. She had been encouraging their eating habits to lean more toward natural and healthy options and had made some progression. So, she grabbed fruits, but also hot dogs and chips.

"Kids are so random with what they eat, aren't they?" a woman commented as Courtney placed a piece of broccoli on Todd's plate.

She laughed and nodded. "And it changes daily!"

"Hi, I'm Lindy. Oscar's wife."

"Hi. I'm Courtney, Brian's girlfriend."

Lindy raised an eyebrow. "Dating the big wig. Wow. I thought he'd never date again."

Smiling, she shrugged. "I guess he changed his mind."

Walking over to her table, she set the plates of food down. Brian walked over to her and kissed her cheek.

"Glad you're here. How's the food look?"

"Everything is great." Glancing past him at the jumpy castle, she smiled. "It's nice there is so much for the kids to do too!"

"Yeah. It's always a good idea to keep the kids busy at these kinds of things. You know?"

"Right." Glancing at Lindy, she directed her attention back on Brian. "I met this gal named Lindy. She didn't have any idea we were dating. Are you not telling people?"

"I tell people when it comes up. Are you okay?" Brian

came closer, his look growing more serious. "I'm not trying to hide you or anything, if that's what you're asking."

"I was just curious."

"Come on, let's go around. I want to introduce you to the crew. You can finally meet the rest of the people who work for me." He put out a hand for her to grab.

Smiling, she took his hand and let him lead the way.

At a little past nine thirty that evening, the sun finally began to set and everyone in attendance, including the children, migrated out to the warehouse bay doors for the fireworks.

As Brian and a few of the warehouse workers set up the fireworks, Courtney tried to settle the boys down in chairs.

"There's going to be fireworks in just a minute. Remember the video I showed you earlier today? With all the colors and explosions?"

Todd was pulling his body away from her, trying to go back in through the bay doors to return to the jumpy castle.

"I want to go jump."

"There's no kids in there. Everyone is out here, buddy."

"But I want to go inside."

Suddenly, a firework shot into the sky. Everyone cheered and Blaze clapped excitedly. Todd screamed and jerked his hand away from Courtney, covering his ears. He started running and Courtney jumped from her seat in pursuit of him.

Finding him in a dimly lit hallway sitting down with his hands over his ears crying, she sat down beside him. Leaning her back against the wall, she could hear the fireworks going off outside in the distance.

She wrapped an arm around Todd and brought him into her hold.

"I don't want to go outside!" he shouted. "It hurts my ears!"

"That's fine. We'll sit right here."

He finally relaxed and let himself lean into her side. Holding him close to her, she let herself enjoy the moment of being there for him.

When it was time to leave after the fireworks, Brian helped Courtney with the boys out to the car. After buckling them into their car seats, she shut the back door and turned toward Brian.

"Sorry the fireworks we got scared Todd." Brian rubbed his neck, appearing to take on the guilt of Todd's fear.

Shaking her head, she leaned in and kissed him as she smiled. "It was fine, Brian. He is just sensitive. We all had a lovely time. Thank you for having us."

He let out a relieved sigh. "Good. I'm glad you still think it went well. You ready for court in a few days?"

Her insides dipped into her stomach. "Ready or not, right?"

Brian nodded and pulled her in close to him, holding her for a moment. "We'll get through it together." Then he kissed her deeply.

CHAPTER 10

*H*ours before court a few days later, Courtney tried to wait patiently for Brian and Susan to arrive at her apartment. He was going with her, and Susan was going to stay with the boys. Today, Courtney would be going to the courthouse to face her sister and mother. She had learned in the last couple of days that her mother, Rhonda, had flown in from Blackfoot, Idaho, to be there as moral support for Taylor.

Courtney's heart and mind were being tossed to and fro in waves of uneasiness in the days leading up to that particular morning. She prayed more than she had ever prayed and kept committing all her anxiety to the Lord, but it wouldn't relent. Hearing the knock on the front door that morning, she rushed to answer it.

It wasn't Brian or Susan. It was her mother, and she did not look pleased.

"Mom?"

Rhonda stepped across the threshold and into the apartment. Turning herself to face Courtney, she glared as she tore into her daughter. "How dare you do this! You are tearing this family apart with this choice! You think your father would be pleased with you right now if he were alive?"

Courtney's thoughts and gaze shifted to the boys in the living room. Hurrying over to them, she ignored her mom and helped them get down to their room to play. Once she shut the door, she returned to the living room. Breathing deeply as she lifted prayers toward Heaven, she came face-to-face with her mother in the living room.

"I'm trying to protect these boys."

"By keeping them from their mother?" She laughed sarcastically. "Wow. You are delusional. Some protector you are!"

Taking a step closer to her mother as the pain continued to pelt against her heart, Courtney shook her head and spoke softly. "*No.* I am keeping them away from drugs and abuse. We both know Drake and what he has done, and we both know they're on meth."

"You don't know that. You haven't even spoken to Taylor since you called the cops on her!"

"I didn't call the cops, Mom. She brought them with her."

Another knock sounded on the door. Peering past her mother at the door, her heart knew it was Brian. Thankfulness washed over her.

"I'm leaving."

Going over to the door, Rhonda pushed by Brian and left but stopped and came back a second later.

"Your days of playing house are over, missy!"

As soon as her mother was gone, Courtney fell into Brian's arms and wept into his shoulder. He didn't speak but instead just held her close as she cried. He smoothed his hand over her hair and rubbed her back lightly. His touch and his presence helped ease the pain the day was already catapulting into Courtney's heart.

"Thank you for coming." Courtney dabbed her eyes with the palm of her hands as she released from holding Brian.

"I'm sorry you have to go through all of this. I can't imagine the heartache that is transpiring inside you right now."

"It's okay." Her eyes shifted toward the hallway and the boys' room. "There's a reason for it."

After Susan arrived a short while later that morning, Courtney and Brian headed to the courthouse. They were early, so they walked a few blocks down from the courthouse and grabbed a coffee.

Sitting down at a table with Brian near a window, she sipped on her caramel latte and looked around nervously, wondering if she'd see her sister or mother nearby.

Reaching a hand over, Brian touched the top of her hand.

"Hey. It's going to be okay."

"You don't know that, Brian. I could lose today. Then what? Then the boys go with her and . . ." Choking up on her words, she paused. "I can't imagine not having them with me and they being with her. The drugs, the abuse."

"You have to trust God. I know it's hard right now, and it'll be hard if things don't work out, but at least you'll know you tried. You stood up for those who can't stand up for themselves."

"Trying doesn't save lives, Brian."

"No, but God doesn't rely on our strength. He only relies on Himself. He just needs us to show up sometimes and be a voice for those who cannot speak. Be His mouthpiece with our concern and our care for those who are weak and who are small. "

"I know."

Slipping her phone out from her purse, she saw it was time to start walking back to the courthouse. Her throat tightened and her breathing became shallow. Fear was keeping every muscle tense in her entire body. Brian must've sensed it because in the next moment, he stood and grabbed her hand, pulling her into his embrace.

"We're going to get through this, no matter what."

Holding onto him, she let out a relieved sigh as more tears fell. *Thank You for him, God,* she prayed.

Walking with Brian back to the courthouse, Courtney tried to focus on her surroundings and stay grounded within the confines of reality. Seeing a bird fly overhead, she kept her eyes on it as it landed on a snow-covered branch in the courtyard of the courthouse buildings. The bird reminded her of a Scripture she had memorized shortly after the passing of her late husband, Drew.

Look at the birds of the air; they do not sow or reap or store away in barns,
and yet your heavenly Father feeds them. Are you not much more valuable than they?
Can any one of you by worrying add a single hour to your life?
Matthew 6:26-27

Her pulse settled a fraction and she felt the warmth and love of God wash over her. Stopping near the tree, she turned to Brian and smiled.

"God is holding me right now." Her eyes went to the steps leading into the courthouse. "I can feel Him."

He smiled and nodded. "He does that. Just keep breathing and you'll get through this."

He took her hand and they walked together up the steps into the courthouse.

Once inside, they found the courtroom and met with the

CPS representative who was handling their case. They sat with him outside of the courtroom doors on a bench. His name was Donny Hinland. He reassured her and Brian that Taylor wouldn't be taking the boys, but ultimately, that decision would be up to the judge. As they were discussing, her mother and sister arrived and went into the courtroom.

"Okay. Let's get in there." Donny opened the door of the courtroom. Courtney and Brian walked toward the door, but Donny stopped Brian. "Family only."

Courtney hugged him for a long moment. "I'll be okay."

"I know you will be. I'll be right out here, praying for you."

"Thank you."

Turning, Courtney went inside the courtroom. Passing wood benches that reminded her of pews from her old church, she followed Donny to a small desk with a microphone and a pitcher of water sitting on top of it. Her sister, Taylor, was on the opposite side of the room with a desk and microphone as well. Taylor had her makeup done and was wearing a dress. By all appearances, she seemed like a perfectly fine person without a drug or abuse issue. Her mother, Rhonda, was sitting in one of the benches behind Taylor.

The judge wasn't in the room.

"All rise." The court bailiff's voice boomed across the room, commanding everyone to stand. As Courtney stood, she peered up at the ceiling and prayed. *God, I leave this all in Your hands. I'm scared, but I trust You.*

WITH HIS HANDS FOLDED AND deep in prayer, Brian prayed over the proceedings unfolding behind the closed door of the courtroom. Forty minutes after Courtney had left to go inside, a distraught and tear-filled Taylor came storming out of the courtroom doors, followed by her mother.

Standing up, Brian watched as the two of them stormed away and down the hallway. His eyes watered and his heart ached as he sat back down and prayed for Taylor and Rhonda. He knew this most likely meant that Courtney would indeed keep the boys, but he also knew the hurt that was in their two hearts in that moment. Praying, he asked God to ease their suffering. *God, please reveal Yourself to Taylor and Rhonda through this. I know Courtney has no desire to keep the children away from their mother, merely a desire to keep the boys safe. Praise You, Lord, for the boys staying safe. Please ease Taylor and Rhonda's heartache on this day, and may they be drawn to the truth and reality before them. I lift my heart up to You with thankfulness for Your deliverance of these children away from harm and into love.*

Fifteen minutes later, Courtney and Donny emerged from the courtroom doors. Teary-eyed and relieved, Courtney fell into his arms.

"I can't believe I doubted for a second." She let out a relieved sigh as she started to cry. "God is so good."

"Amen. What'd the judge say?"

"That I have guardianship permanently, but Taylor can dissolve it if she proves to the courts that she has somewhere for the boys to stay and shows that her life is stable and together. I told the judge I'd personally dissolve it if she proves to be stable."

Donny added. "Aside from being in rehab, admitting to drug use in the last thirty days, and the hospital records of abuse by her current boyfriend, the biggest problem for her was the fact that she had no real place of her own to keep the boys. Her boyfriend lives in a shared apartment and has no dedicated room for the boys to stay in, and Rhonda's house is only a studio in Blackfoot." He shrugged. "If she gets her life in order, she can get them back."

Brian nodded. "Which is great if she does."

Courtney smiled. "Yes. I just want to protect them."

Walking together out to the car, Brian opened the passenger-side door for her. As she climbed in, he could see a different woman from the one he had encountered that morning. She seemed more relaxed. Rounding the car, he got in and they headed back to her apartment.

"How'd my mom and sister seem on their way out?"

"Pretty upset."

Courtney peered out her window. "I really need to make amends with them. I just don't know how. They disagree with me so strongly, but I know it needs to be resolved at some point."

"You have to give it over to God and let Him work on their hearts." He thought about Melissa, about his own harboring of bitterness. "Maybe with time, you can talk with them."

Courtney sighed heavily. "Yeah. They say time heals all wounds, but . . . my mother isn't like that. She's different, Brian. I'm worried."

"Don't worry. Trust. You learned that today. Right?"

Smiling over at him, she nodded. "Yes, I did. Hey. Have you talked to Melissa yet?"

He shook his head. "No. What would I say?"

"If you forgive her, you should tell her."

"Maybe I will. Maybe I should ask her for forgiveness for the way I've acted too."

She smiled. "Yeah."

Arriving back at the apartment, Courtney stayed in the living room with Susan and talked about court while Brian went down the hallway to the boys' bedroom. Pushing open the door the rest of the way, he saw that they had stacked books atop one another and made a ramp for their cars, just like the one he had shown them. He smiled.

"Brian!" they exclaimed as they jumped up and ran over to him, wrapping their little arms around his legs.

"Hey, guys. Building a ramp, huh?"

He sat down with them and raced their little cars up and down the ramp. Then he read them a few stories from the stack under the ramp. As he finished a story and set the book back onto the stack, he thought again about Melissa, about Courtney's encouragement to deal with the feelings he had stored up in bitterness toward his ex-wife. Rising from the boys' floor, he went out into the living room. Susan had just left.

"Hey."

"Hi." Courtney came over and wrapped her arms around him.

"I'm going to go talk to Melissa."

"All right. I'll be praying."

Getting in his car, he prayed on his way over to Melissa and Conrad's house. Pulling up to the curb, he peered over at the triple-story house they had bought with the settlement money from the divorce. *I don't even know what I'm going to say. I should leave.* He went to turn the key over to leave when Conrad opened the front door and waved.

His insides twisted. Brian realized he had more unforgiveness than he had first thought. He hated Conrad more than his ex-wife for what happened. He had trusted Conrad and let him into his home, into his life. Then Conrad took advantage of the situation and took his wife away from him.

Closing his eyes, Brian breathed in truths of God and exhaled the hate inside his heart. Getting out of the car, he headed up the sidewalk toward Conrad.

They struck hands, firmly shaking.

"What's up, Brian? It's not your weekend, is it? Wait, it's only Wednesday."

He shook his head. "No, I think we need to talk."

Raising his eyebrows, Conrad shrugged. "Sure. Let's talk. Come on inside."

Walking with Conrad, Brian could feel his heart pounding in his chest as he crossed over the threshold into the house. Pictures of Melissa and his daughter flooded the entryway, making what he was attempting to do not the least bit easier. Conrad led them into the kitchen and to the table.

They sat down.

"So, Brian. What do you want to talk about?"

"I want to let you know that I forgive you, and I want to ask your forgiveness too."

Furrowing his eyebrows, Conrad shook his head. "For what?"

"For the way I have been treating you. I never let go of what happened and I have mistreated you."

"I didn't realize that, but thanks."

Taking in Conrad's words, Brian realized it was true. Holding unforgiveness in his own heart only had an impact on him, not on the other person. Conrad hadn't even noticed.

"Is Melissa around?"

"Sure, she's up in her office. I'll go get her."

Conrad left the room and then suddenly, Lucy came in the kitchen's back door.

"Dad?"

"Hey, Princess."

"What are you doing here?" She took off her gloves and walked over to the table.

"I'm just here talking to your mother and Conrad."

Melissa entered the kitchen cautiously, looking confused

just as much as Conrad did, if not more. "Hi, Brian. Conrad said you wanted to talk?"

"Yes."

"Come on into the front room and we'll chat there."

He followed his ex-wife into the front room. "Hey. Thanks for talking to me. I wanted to let you know that I forgive you, and also, I want to apologize for the way I've behaved. I haven't been very nice and I just want to say I'm sorry."

"You're not forgiven."

Looking around for a moment as confusion set into his mind, he shook his head. "What?"

"I said you're not forgiven. You've made me go through so much punishment after everything happened. I don't forgive you."

"Okay." He knew God's forgiveness wasn't dependent on hers, so he tried to not let it hurt, even though it did sting. "Thanks for letting me talk to you."

"Sure. I'll walk you out."

Melissa followed behind him. At the door, he turned toward her and caught sight of Lucy in the hallway a few feet behind her. He shot a wave at her, but Melissa slammed the door.

His heart ached in that moment. He hadn't known he had caused Melissa so much pain, but it was apparent now that he had. Brian had always demonized her and made every-thing about how she had hurt him. Now he realized he had hurt her too. Peering up at the cold winter sky on the way back to his car, he cried out to God. "Forgive me, Lord! Oh, how blind I am to my own sins and my own shortcomings. Heal my heart and drive out this bitterness. Only You can fix this wicked heart of mine!"

Arriving at his house a short while later, he went inside

and shut the door behind him. The house was quiet and he was alone in his thoughts.

Walking into the living room, he sat down on the couch and retrieved his Bible from the coffee table. Opening it up, he read for a while in 1 Timothy. Upon arriving at the second chapter, he read the first four verses and then stopped.

I urge, then, first of all, that petitions, prayers, intercession and
thanksgiving be made for all people—
for kings and all those in authority, that we may live peaceful and
quiet lives in all godliness and holiness.
This is good, and pleases God our Savior,
who wants all people to be saved and to come to a knowledge of the
truth.
1 Timothy 2:1-4

He thought about his earlier conversation with Melissa. He thought about how he hadn't prayed for her once since they divorced. Closing his Bible, he went his knees and folded his hands together and rested them on the coffee table. "God, I lift up my ex-wife to You, Lord. Only You understand that woman. May she find her way back to a relationship with You, God. Her peace and joy seem to have gone from her, and I pray that it returns." Wiping tears from his cheeks as he paused for a moment, he knew his prayer was real because he could feel it within his bones. He went on. "And I pray for Conrad. I pray that You prosper his hands and every bit of work he does as a restaurant supply consultant. I pray that You bring this family to You, Lord. Show them Your glorious light and Your ways. I lift up their life, their marriage, and their family. Amen."

AFTER PUTTING THE BOYS TO bed that evening, Courtney slipped the stack of prayer journals Drew had written from the desk drawer in the boys' bedroom and brought them out to the living room.

Opening one, she flipped through it and stopped.

9/1/2010

Bible reading: 2 Thessalonians 1-3

Focus: In the final chapter of Thessalonians two verses struck me right in the heart. It was in verses four and five. 'We have confidence in the Lord that you are doing and will continue to do the things we command. May the Lord direct your hearts into God's love and Christ's perseverance.' It struck me for a particular reason. Two days ago, I was informed that my grandmother has about five months to live. My heart is broken, but I know that I will continue to do what is right and will continue to be directed by the Lord. May her new residence in Heaven be nothing short of divine.

Prayers:

I'd like to begin prayers today focused on my wife. It seems to me that she seems more upset than I do about my grandmother's declining health. I know she has become attached to her since we've been spending more time in Idaho Falls. Lord, please ease the discomfort my wife feels in her heart. Let her be focused on Your peace, Your love, Your goodness in her life. Help me be of good encouragement to her.

Just then, a knock sounded on Courtney's apartment door,

interrupting her time in the journal. Closing the journal, she placed it along with the others in a drawer inside the coffee table.

Going over to the door, she checked the peephole. It was her mother, Rhonda.

Seeing tears running down her cheeks and a look of sadness clouding her expression, Courtney's heart was moved with compassion.

Unlatching the lock, she opened the door.

"Mom?"

With trembling lips, she shook her head. "Courtney, can we talk?"

"Yes. Come in."

Letting her mother come into the apartment, the two of them sat down at the kitchen table.

"I had no idea that Taylor would lose today. I thought she was doing all the right things, but when that judge explained it, it clicked. I hope you can forgive me."

Moved deeply by her words, Courtney nodded and grabbed her mother's hand with a gentle touch. She realized she had forgiven her mother already, even after the way she had sided against her in court and flipped out on her that same morning. Courtney's heart was in a constant flow of forgiveness for all the hurt she felt. "Mom. I love you and I love Taylor. I never wanted a battle. I only wanted what was best for these boys. I'm trying to do what is best."

"Will you at least let me see them?"

"Of course, and Taylor can too once she's clean and stable. I'd prefer for her not to be with Drake, but I can't do much about that."

"Really?" Rhonda's eyes filled with more tears. "Even after all that she did to you?"

"Absolutely."

"How can you be so quick to forgive?"

Shaking her head, she smiled. "Look at all the Lord has forgiven me of, Mom. I can't help but love and forgive."

Standing up, she came closer to Courtney and hugged her. "I love you, Daughter. You have a greater faith in God than I."

"Would you like some tea?"

"Yes. I'd love that." Rhonda wiped her eyes as Courtney went over to the stove and put on a kettle of water. "Does Taylor have a plan?"

"She does. I'm relocating to Spokane, and she's going to live with me in a three-bedroom apartment while she does outpatient treatment. Then she'll get a job and whatnot. She wants to be close to the boys so she can see them when she's sober."

"That's a great plan."

Pouring cups of hot, steamy water, Courtney dropped a tea bag into each mug and brought them over to the kitchen table along with cream and sugar. Sitting down, she placed a couple of lumps of sugar into her tea.

"Still two lumps."

"*Always.*" Wanting to know more about Taylor, Courtney gently touched against the subject. "So, where is Taylor now?"

"She's at the hotel."

"Drake?"

"She's not with him now. They broke up this afternoon following court. She realized he was seriously holding her back."

"I hope she sticks with that." Taking a sip of her tea, Courtney's heart worried about Taylor. "I don't understand why she started getting with terrible men."

"It was after your father died that she did. Remember that nice fellow she was dating back before Frank passed . . . what's his name?"

"Ralph? I remember him."

"Yes! *Ralph.* Once Frank passed away, Ralph pushed her away hard, and she went to the first guy who showed her any kind of affection, and then a different one after that. The rest is history."

"That's so sad. Did anyone figure out why Ralph did that?"

She shook her head. "No."

Courtney peered over toward the hallway and thought about the boys. "But we wouldn't have Blaze and Todd if it didn't all happen to work out the way it did."

"God works all things together for good for those who love Him and are called according to His purpose." Rhonda peered over at the hallway. "That Todd is smart. Both of them are smart, but that Todd seems beyond his little two-year-old self. You know?"

"I know." Courtney's heart warmed with love as she sat with her mother in the kitchen that night. It was truly a miracle of God, the transformation that had taken place in their relationship from that early morning to that evening.

CHAPTER 11

*I*n early February, Brian met with Edgar Tomchak, the veterinarian nutritionist he hired for each new line of dog food. He discussed with him his desires to introduce a line of dog food that boosts energy while remaining nutritional. Costco had been loving the line of dog food in their store so far but wanted something new and fresh.

"It'll take some time for us to perfect a new balanced formula, but I think it's absolutely possible. You have testers lined up?"

"Yes." Brian smiled. "The same people and their dogs from the last time. They love being a part of the testing process and they love the free dog food."

"Great. Then we'll start Monday." Standing up in Brian's office at the warehouse, Edgar reached a hand over the desk.

Brian stood and they shook hands.

After leaving the warehouse, Brian's phone rang in the car. Pressing the answer button on the car's dashboard, he answered.

"Hey, Brian. It's me, April. My phone died and I'm using my daughter's cell phone to call you. I am still planning to show up tonight, but I'm running a few minutes behind. Will 6:15 PM work?"

"Yes, my reservation is for seven PM. You didn't mention anything at the ladies' Bible study last night?"

She laughed. "No! I kept my lips sealed. She's going to love the surprise. See you soon."

"Thanks again for this! I really appreciate it, and I know Courtney will too."

"No problem at all. Courtney works so hard for those boys and loves on them unconditionally. She deserves a night out! See you soon."

"'Bye."

Hanging up, Brian lifted a prayer of thanks up to God. *Lord, You are so good to me, to us. Thank You for placing people into my life who reflect Your love. Amen.*

Parking at the apartment complex, he shut off the car and peered through the windshield toward Courtney's apartment. She thought they were just going to have a relaxing evening at her apartment with the boys. Maybe watch a movie after the boys go to sleep and that was it. She had no idea the plans Brian had made with April to watch the boys so he could take her out.

Getting to the door, he knocked.

She opened the door.

"Come on in." She had Blaze on her hip, and he was crying.

He stepped across the threshold and gave her a peck on her lips.

"What's going on, little guy?" Brian took Blaze into his arms and rubbed his back, attempting to calm him down.

"He and Todd were roughhousing around, and he got hurt." Courtney went into the kitchen and turned the dial on the soup down to low. "I'm trying to finish up dinner. It's your favorite, soup."

She was joking, knowing that he didn't care for soup of any kind. "Mmm. Sounds good."

Laughing, she looked over as she gave the pot a stir. "You don't have to lie."

"Your soups are growing on me a little."

Setting the ladle into the soup, she wiped her hands on a hand towel hanging from the stove. "It's time to eat. I'll go get Todd."

Blaze had calmed down and Brian set him down. Just as Courtney was about to enter the hallway to head down to the spare room, the doorbell rang.

"Who could that be?"

Brian broke into a grin. "I have a surprise for you."

Walking over to the door, Brian opened it and it was April.

"What? I'm confused. What are you doing here, April?"

"I'm here to relieve you so you can go out with Brian tonight."

Courtney's eyes widened as she came over to Brian and April near the door. "What? Really?"

"Yes. You know I won't be around for a while coming up as I'm working with Edgar at the warehouse, and I want to treat you out before things get hectic."

"All right. Awesome. Thank you! Both of you! Let me go get ready!"

———

DOLLED UP AND READY FOR the surprise date with Brian, Courtney sat in the passenger seat of his car. She felt weird.

"It's so strange to not have the boys in the backseat." She laughed. "I feel like I'm in an alternate reality or something. I mean, court was different. This is a date!"

"I bet it feels a little different. You've spent every moment with them for months now. It's time to relax for an evening."

"What do you have planned?"

"You'll have to wait and see."

He drove to downtown Spokane and parked outside the Clinkerdagger, an upscale restaurant overlooking the Spokane River. As they sat down at the candlelit table, she felt love and warmth washing over her entire body.

"You're so sweet to me, Brian."

"It's easy being sweet to a woman like you."

"Aw." She clasped her heart pendant necklace as her heart melted. "It's hard to see how I'm doing anything right sometimes when the boys are so difficult. The blessing is they're not that way at your house at all."

"Which is awesome, otherwise I'd have to fire you." They both laughed. "I'm just playing. You really are an amazing person for what you're doing with those boys. I admire you."

"Thanks."

The waitress came over and they ordered their food and drinks. Then they both handed her the menus. As she walked away from the table, Courtney thought about Serenah from the ladies' Bible study. She had started as a waitress in a new town and ended up as a pastor's wife and running multiple businesses.

"Do you ever wonder what the meaning is in all the stuff life throws at us?"

"Absolutely, I do."

"Me too. I have to remind myself that it's God who has the full picture of our life. He knows where we are going, and He is the one who can lead us in the direction we should go." Reminded of Melody, she shook her head. "But sometimes, tragedy happens. Like with Drew, or this lady at my Bible study. She lost her daughter."

Brian paused for a moment, shaking his head. He took a

drink of his ice water and set it down on the table. "Life is uncertain sometimes and can change in a moment, but God never changes. He is the same, always and forever. I find that comforting."

Courtney nodded. "I love that He doesn't change."

After dinner, they braved the chilly air and went for a stroll in Riverfront Park. They walked for a while, then sat down on the frozen cement steps near the waterfront.

"I love who I am when I'm with you."

Courtney smiled over at him. "Yeah? I love who I am when I'm with you, too."

She scooted closer to him and snuggled into his hold. He leaned in and kissed her gently. Deepening the kiss, he adjusted, holding her close to him. Warmth rushed from her head to her toes and filled her entire body.

After a few minutes, they released from kissing. Holding her in his arms as they shared the view of the river, he asked about her sister. "How's your sister doing with sobriety? Hanging in there?"

"Yes. She's still clean. My mother seems hopeful, and so am I."

He nodded. "That's good. How's your heart doing with all that? I mean, I couldn't imagine having the boys for this long and then seeing the possible end in sight in the coming months and days."

"It's hard, but it's a mixed bag of emotions. I'd love to see the old Taylor come back to us fully and stay. I'm hesitant to believe, but I'm praying it's lasting and true."

"It's kind of like what we were talking about back at the restaurant. God having the big picture in mind. We have to keep reminding ourselves of that. Especially in this situation."

"Absolutely." Turning her gaze up at him, she smiled. "You're so cute with the boys, Brian. I love it."

He smiled. "I love them. Sure, they're difficult at times, but they're precious gifts from God, and I couldn't imagine life without them and without you."

Arriving back home that evening, and after Brian and April left, Courtney ventured down to the boys' bedroom door. Opening the door quietly, she went in and kissed each of their foreheads.

Brian was right. These boys were gifts from God and Courtney knew it. If it wasn't for their coming into her life and into her heart, she wouldn't have known the joy of giving unconditional love, and for that reason among many others, she was eternally thankful to God.

CHAPTER 12

*T*he snow and ice began to melt in March, the following month. The early signs of spring had arrived in Spokane and winter was over. It wasn't just the winter that was coming to a conclusion, but the month-long project Brian had been working on with Edgar. He had been working long hours at the warehouse in town, trying to perfect the new recipe of dog food for the spring roll out. By the end of March, it was finally complete.

"This is going to be great dog food." Edgar patted the cylinder of the first batch. "Each and every dog owner has reported increased energy levels in their pups."

"I'm excited."

"Excited enough to get another dog?"

Brian laughed and shook his head. "Nah. I'm okay for now without one. Come by the house tomorrow and I'll cut you a final check. Great job, Edgar." Shaking hands with Edgar outside the warehouse that evening, Brian went to his car and got in.

Breathing a relieved sigh to be done with the new formula, he peered up at the ceiling of his car and prayed.

"Thank You, God. I couldn't be running this business without You by my side and You bringing these people into my life. It truly takes a small army to run a business, and I thank You for all the people You place in my life. Amen."

Arriving home, Brian went to the shower to wash off the smell of dog food. As the hot water crashed over his head, he had flashes of Courtney flip through his mind. He hadn't been seeing much of her during the last two months since he'd started working with Edgar on the formula. They still made sure to make time for each other at least a couple of nights a week, but it hadn't been the same as it was back in the first few months when she started.

Shutting off the shower, he got dressed in a pair of sweats, a white T-shirt, and a hoodie, then went into his living room and turned on the television.

An hour went by and then his phone rang. Glancing at the screen on his cell, he saw it was her.

"Courtney."

"Hey. I put your dinner on the second shelf in the fridge. Don't forget to eat."

He smiled and tossed the remote on the cushion beside him. "You know me too well."

"I sure do. Did Edgar sign off on it today?"

"Yes! *Finally.* I was beginning to think we'd never get this formula done." Opening the refrigerator, he saw the container of dinner she had prepared. Pulling it out, he took it over to the island and popped the red Tupperware lid off. Steak, potatoes, and carrots. "Thanks for the food."

Turning around, he set it in the microwave and pressed two minutes.

"You're welcome. Taylor called today."

"Oh, yeah?" Raising his eyebrows, he leaned against the island. "How'd that go?"

"Good. She asked about the boys and wanted to hear all

about how they were doing in school. She's been sober since court three months ago now."

Sensing the distress in her tone, Brian furrowed his eyebrows. "That's not a good thing?"

"It is. I'm just worried, and I just . . ."

"You've grown attached." He raised his eyebrows. "Can't say I blame you. I'm guilty of that too."

"These boys are in my life day in and day out, you know?" She was quiet on the other end of the phone for a moment but then let out a heavy sigh. "But that's okay. I know God will get me through this. That and I have this amazing boyfriend."

"Oh?" He smiled, raising an eyebrow. "Is he nice?"

She laughed. "He's all right."

The microwave dinged. "There's my dinner. I'll see you in the morning?"

"Bright and early. See you in the morning."

WHILE WORKING ON REPLYING TO emails in Brian's inbox the next morning, Courtney kept her eyes on Blaze who was lying on the small sofa in the room. He had been running a low-grade fever that morning and had a sore throat. Seeing Blaze try to get up off the couch, she scooted her office chair away from the desk and went over to him. Bending a knee beside him at the couch, she smoothed a hand over his face and pushed his hair back away from his forehead. Kissing his forehead, she could tell the fever was subsiding.

"Just try to rest, bud."

Just then, Brian walked into the room.

"Hey."

Courtney stood up and went into the hallway with Brian.

"I have to run down to the warehouse. The new formula

is working great, but the new freezer we just got in a few days ago is having issues. I have to go see what's up."

"Okay. Have fun with that."

His eyes went to the doorway. "Is Blaze okay?"

"Yeah. Just feeling a little under the weather."

"Well, you can go home if you need to. I'd totally understand."

"I'll monitor him. It's okay for now."

"All right. By the way, if you're here at about ten o'clock, Edgar will be coming by to pick up a check. I left it on the kitchen island in case I'm not back in a couple of hours. Could you give it to him?"

"Sure."

"Great." Leaning in, he kissed her cheek and then left.

Working through the inbox took a good chunk of time that morning. Then it was time to organize hard copies of the most recent invoices. She worked on sorting and organizing invoices when suddenly, the doorbell chimes sounded. Todd jumped up and Blaze did too. Checking the time on her cell phone, she saw it was already eleven, an hour past ten.

"Who's that?" Todd inquired, coming closer to her and latching onto her leg.

She smiled at him. "Probably Edgar, Brian's work partner. You want to go with me to see him?"

"Yes."

"Me too!" Blaze hurried over to her. She scooped him into her arms and all three of them ventured down the hall to go meet Edgar at the door.

Opening the door, she greeted Edgar and led him inside.

"I haven't seen you in a while."

"Not since I brought my puppy, Max, over a couple of months ago for dinner. Do you boys want to see him again? He's grown a lot!" He pointed toward his truck. "He came along with me."

"Yes!" Todd shouted.

He looked at Courtney for approval.

"Yeah, that's fine."

Edgar ran out to his truck while Courtney and the boys went into the kitchen. Picking up the check, she turned toward the entryway, waiting for Edgar. Barking flooded her ears as Edgar brought him inside and into the kitchen. Max jumped onto Todd, causing his steps to falter.

"Down, Max. Down!" Edgar scolded him. Max lowered his head, wagging his tail as both Todd and Blaze patted his side and head.

Edgar came over to Courtney.

"Here you go." She handed him the check, and he folded it, shoving it into his coat pocket.

"Thanks."

"Do you want some coffee? We were about to have a snack. I made blueberry muffins earlier this morning."

"I'd love a snack. I haven't eaten at all!" Edgar popped himself on a stool at the island while Courtney warmed up muffins with butter inside them. Pouring a cup of coffee for Edgar, she brought the muffin and mug over to him. As she set it down, the front door opened.

Walking over to the kitchen entryway, she peeked in the foyer at Brian.

"Hey. Edgar is here."

He raised an eyebrow and nodded as he kicked his shoes off. She came back into the kitchen.

Brian arrived a moment later, slipping his hand along her lower back. Her smile grew as he pulled her in and kissed her. Then he went over to Edgar and shook his hand.

"What's up, Edgar?" Brian peered at his coffee and muffin. "You eating my food and drinking my coffee?"

Edgar smiled with a laugh to his tone. "Why, yes, I am."

"Maybe you should leave."

Edgar's smile fell away. "What?"

"I said, maybe you should leave."

Touching Brian's arm, Courtney shook her head. "Why are you acting like this?"

Edgar nodded and stood up from the stool. "I do need to get going. I have a lot going on." Patting his coat pocket, he flashed a quick smile toward Brian. "Thanks again."

Edgar grabbed Max by the collar and walked him out of the kitchen and to the door. Brian accompanied him. Courtney stayed in the kitchen, mulling over in her mind what the problem might be with him. Then, she remembered his past. Touching her mouth with a hand, she shook her head. *No. He doesn't think that.*

The front door slammed shut, and she jumped, startled by the sound. Turning, she looked at the kitchen entryway, but Brian didn't come back in. Courtney took the boys to her office and then went to find Brian.

Arriving at his office door, she found it shut.

She knocked.

"I'm busy."

She turned the knob and went in anyway.

He turned toward her, spinning his chair to face her. Opening his arms wide, he shrugged. "I guess the words '*I'm busy*' don't matter to you."

"Stop."

"Stop what? Being busy? I have a company to run and—"

She reached out and touched his arm. "*Brian.*"

He peered up at her.

"I'm not Melissa. I'm not going to hurt you like she did."

"I just don't like finding men in my house. I said to hand him the check, not invite him to stay all day and play house in my home."

"Stop. This is because you're insecure and you fear me doing what your ex-wife did."

"How dare you! I didn't tell you that so you could throw it in my face!" He turned away, directing his attention to his computer.

Floodwaters of hurt rose within Courtney's heart. Her eyes began to water and she backed away slowly from him. He didn't take his eyes off the computer screen as she made it to the door. Turning, she left his office.

As Courtney walked down the hallway, she wiped tears from her cheeks. Brian, for the first time since knowing him, had hurt her. He didn't just feel closed off. He felt as if he were . . . dead.

She grabbed the boys and left his house.

———

AT A LITTLE PAST TWO o'clock that afternoon, some hours later, Brian left his office to go get lunch. Walking out into the kitchen, he listened for Courtney and the boys down the hall in her office.

It was silent.

Walking down the hall, he peeked inside her office.

Nobody was there.

Walking back down the hall, he went into the living room and peered out into the back yard.

Nobody.

A sinking feeling came over Brian as he went into the kitchen. He thought about earlier that day and how he had been harsh with her. A passage of Scripture floated to the tip of his mind.

Husbands, love your wives and do not be harsh with them.
Colossians 3:19

Well, she's not my wife, he thought to himself sharply. Walking over to the refrigerator, he opened it and pulled the carton of orange juice out. Taking a long swig, he wiped his lips and set it back on the shelf inside. He saw the leftover lasagna sitting on the second shelf. He recalled her making it three days ago and how it had been the first time in a week since he'd had time with her. *I missed her so much in that week . . .*

He grabbed the leftovers and tossed them into the microwave. As the wheel churned inside the microwave to cook his food, his mind churned as well.

I love her.

The microwave dinged, indicating that his food was done.

Removing his food, he grabbed a fork from the silverware drawer and sat down on the stool Edgar had been sitting on when he arrived home earlier. He recalled adrenaline shooting through his body when he arrived home to see Edgar in his home with Courtney. He thought about Courtney's words in his office—"I'm not Melissa."

Setting his fork down, he leaned his elbow on the island and rubbed his forehead. *What have I done?*

After Brian finished eating, he went into the living room and sat down on the couch. He grabbed his Bible from the coffee table. Pausing before he read, he bowed his head and prayed.

"God. I love that woman and I'm scared to death. I know I shouldn't fear, for fear is but an absence of trust in You. Help me to not compare Courtney to Melissa. Aid me in my efforts to weave through the emotional pain of the past. Weed out the roots of fear that still reside in my heart and wash me, Lord, in Your everlasting love. And please comfort Courtney, Lord." His eyes moistened as he paused, thinking of the harshness he had used with her and how he had shut her out. "It had to hurt the way I acted earlier toward her. Forgive me, Lord. Amen."

Opening his Bible, he started to read in Psalms chapter seven. He read until chapter nine, two verses in.

I will give thanks to you, Lord, with all my heart;
I will tell of all your wonderful deeds.
I will be glad and rejoice in you;
I will sing the praises of your name, O Most High.
Psalm 9:1-2

He lifted his eyes toward the ceiling. "Let my heart be a heart that is thankful toward You always, Lord. You have been so gracious and kind and merciful with me. Let my life sing of Your wonderful deeds. I needed someone just like Courtney, and You brought her into my life. I thought it was just for my business in the beginning, but it has been so much more than that. Thank You!"

He set his Bible down on the coffee table and rose to his feet. Exiting the living room, he went and grabbed his car keys and coat.

On the way to her apartment, he prayed again. "That fear was a lie and was not from You. Help me to be the man of God You want me to be and push that fear away. Let fear be a four-letter word, not only to my vocabulary but to my heart. Let Your power and Your strength and Your love be the cornerstone of my life, Lord."

He called and apologized to Edgar on his way to Courtney's apartment.

Pulling into the apartment complex, his heart dipped when he saw her car parked. Seeing her car reminded him that she had to drive home with a broken heart that he had given her. He parked next to her car and paused before getting out. "Forgive me, Lord. Forgive this wicked heart of mine. Oh, how I struggle to do what is right in this fleshly body! Let my words only be grace, love, and mercy, always. Let Yourself flow through me."

Getting out of his car, he walked to the apartment door and knocked.

The door unlocked and she opened it.

Seeing tears rolling down her cheeks, he crossed the threshold and embraced her.

"I'm so sorry, Courtney!"

"I forgive you, but that's not why I'm crying." Releasing from their embrace, she moved to let him inside.

Raising an eyebrow as he walked in, his gaze stayed locked on her. "What's going on?"

"Tomorrow, the boys will start seeing Taylor." The two of them walked over to the couch in the living room and sat down as she continued. "She's been clean for months and has a job. I know it's time. I just got off the phone with Taylor and my mother."

Opening his arms, he embraced her in a long hug. "God will get you through this."

"I know." Releasing from their hug, she let out a heavy sigh and then dabbed her eyes of the tears. "It's going to be hard, but it's going to be good. Those boys need to be with their mother."

"Plus, you'll still see them. Right? They're staying in town?"

She smiled. "Yes. Those two little dudes have a part of my heart now, so no matter where they go or what they do, I'll be a part of their lives."

Brian smiled at her selfless love. "You truly do love them fully."

"Yes, I do. Even if they're not with me." She stood up. "Want some tea?"

"Let me make it." Brian stood up and went into the kitchen. Looking toward the living room as he set the kettle on the stove, he thought about earlier that morning and how he had acted. "I think we need to talk about this morning."

He came back to Courtney at the couch and sat down fully turned toward her.

"I was harsh with you, and that wasn't right."

"I get what happened. You were just freaked out because of what Melissa did. It's okay."

"*No.*" Brian rested a hand atop hers. "It's not okay. Yes, it was due to my past hurt, but it isn't fair to you and it wasn't right."

"You've told me before that you were pushing against the feelings inside that compared me to Melissa, so I can't say it wasn't unexpected. Don't be so hard on yourself."

Shaking his head, Brian looked her in the eyes. "I don't want to break your heart. I don't want to hurt you. Courtney, I love you."

Courtney's lips curled into a smile. "I love you too."

Brian leaned in and touched her cheek softly as he kissed her. Deepening the kiss, he brought his hand down and pulled her in closer to him. Her lips against his felt like being transported to a different world. A world where only they and their love existed.

The kettle on the stovetop whistled, interrupting the moment. Pulling back slowly, he smiled.

"Two lumps of sugar?"

She smiled. "Yes."

He stood up and went into the kitchen. Pouring the hot, steamy water into the two cups, he glanced over to see Courtney at the bookshelves. He placed the tea bags into the cups of water to let them steep and went over to her and the open book. Slipping a hand to her lower back, he came in close and looked down at the pages. Images of Todd and Blaze filled scrapbooking pages.

Pointing one out as she smiled, she glanced at Brian. "That was our first trip to the dentist. Terrible experience, but you can't tell that from the photographs."

Brian smiled. "What happened?"

"Todd wouldn't let the dentist look in his mouth. He just sat there with his mouth closed, refusing to open it."

Raising his eyebrows, Brian shook his head. "What'd you do?"

She laughed. "I bribed him with a sucker. It's funny. Before these boys came into my life, I thought bribery was evil, but it really gets kids without any discipline and structure to listen. At least in the beginning. I don't always bribe them, but it was a good starting path. At least for me in my own experience."

Courtney closed the scrapbook and placed it back on the shelf. Turning toward Brian, she smiled somberly. "I always knew they'd go back to her. That's why I made the scrapbook."

"It's a nice gift to her. She can see all the growing they've done since they have been with you. You know?"

"Yeah."

Brian went into the kitchen to get their tea. Walking back into the living room with their cups a moment later, he saw her with a big smile on her face.

Handing her a cup, he raised an eyebrow. "What are you smiling about?"

"You." She took the cup and came in closer to him. She leaned up and kissed him. "God sent you into my life at the perfect time, Brian Dunlap. Earlier, it wouldn't have worked and later would've been too late. It was the exact right time."

"I feel the same way with you." Leaning in, he kissed her.

CHAPTER 13

*B*y June, the boys had started staying overnight with their mother at the apartment she and Rhonda had rented in the Spokane Valley. While it was hard, especially at first, Courtney was growing more and more comfortable with the progress and transition of the boys back to their mother. The months of visitation, stability in Taylor, and Courtney's unrelenting giving of the matter over to God eased the pain that was ever-present in her heart. She loved the boys and knew her love for them gave her the strength she needed to see this through until the end.

In the second week of August, on Thursday, Courtney went down to the courthouse and filed the petition to terminate her guardianship, thus restoring parental rights of the boys to Taylor. With Brian by her side and a trembling hand holding the pen, she signed her name on the document and handed it to the county clerk. Turning toward Brian, she pressed in against his chest, letting his arms and love wrap around her in that moment.

Walking out of the courthouse and down the steps

moments later, she paused at the base of the steps and turned toward Brian.

"Am I doing the right thing here?"

He smiled and nodded as he gently grabbed both of her arms. "Absolutely."

"Then why do I feel so scared?"

"It's a big deal. Big deals are scary. You've seen Taylor be clean and consistent over these last five months, and there's nothing left to do but what you've done now."

Wiping a stray tear from her cheek, she peered back up the steps of the court building. "I know, but I can't help but worry she could slip right back into the drugs and abuse."

"She could very well do that. But listen." Brian raised his eyebrows and focused on her eyes in the moment. "You have to trust God and trust that this will all work out. You loved those boys and cared for them like they were your own when you had them. Now it's time to keep caring and keep loving, but at a distance."

Falling forward into his arms and his embrace, Courtney clung to Brian's dress shirt he was wearing. "I love you."

Smoothing a hand over her head, he comforted her in that moment. She got a whiff of his cologne, which was no longer just a nice smelling fragrance in her life but a comfort and a surety that everything was going to be okay, no matter what. She loved him deeply and couldn't imagine him not in her life.

"I love you too, Courtney. Let's head over to your sister and mom's place and drop that box off."

"Okay." Releasing from their embrace, they walked over to the parking lot and got into Brian's car. The boys had been staying over at their mother's apartment for almost a whole week now.

Upon arriving at the apartment, Rhonda let them in. The boys were sitting on the couch reading books as

Courtney and Brian entered. She set the box down on the end table.

"Courtney!" the boys shouted in unison when they caught sight of her. Leaping off the couch, they tossed their books on the floor and rushed over to her.

Bending down at her knees, she embraced Todd and Blaze warmly. "How are you guys doing?"

"Good! Mom is at work. But she got us new books! Want to see?" Todd pointed over to the books lying on the carpet in the living room by the couch.

"Yes, I'd love to see them!" Todd took her by the hand and led her over. Opening the books one at a time, he showed her every page. Her heart radiated warmth and love as he detailed each page's illustration to her. He couldn't read the words, but he could explain the pictures.

After spending a few minutes with the boys, she sat with Brian and Rhonda at the kitchen table.

"Well, I was hoping I would see Taylor. I forgot she worked today. I signed the petition today and turned it in to the court."

Rhonda smiled. "Awesome. Might as well. They've been here for a week now. They seem like they're feeling the 'home' vibe these days."

"Yeah, it was time." Courtney's gaze fell to Todd and Blaze as they were now wrestling on the floor in the living room.

"I don't think I've told you this, Courtney." Rhonda paused, seeming to get choked up in the moment.

Turning her gaze toward her mother, she raised an eyebrow. "Told me what?"

"Thank you. Truly, thank you for taking the boys in when she went to rehab, and thank you for keeping them even when I was pressuring you otherwise. Taylor would've never gotten to where she is today if it weren't for you."

"You're welcome." Courtney had wanted to hear those

words for a long time, yet now, when it was the furthest thing from her desires and from her mind, it was when her mother spoke them. For Courtney, a thank you no longer mattered to her because she had let go of the pain, had forgiven the trespasses done to her and relinquished all care of herself in the matter. All she cared about was the boys and their wellbeing. All she cared about was their getting the love and care they needed.

TAKING COURTNEY BACK TO HER apartment after visiting with the boys and Rhonda, Brian went inside with her. Shutting the door behind him, he watched as Courtney went over to the couch. Her movements were slow, and he could sense some measure of pain within her from the day's events down at the courthouse. It was hard for him to see her sign the petition, so he knew it had to be worlds more difficult for her.

Coming around the side of the couch, he sat down beside her.

"You all right?"

She smiled softly and looked over at him. "Yeah, I'm okay."

Brian's phone rang. It was a call from the warehouse. Standing up, he walked over into the kitchen.

"Hey. One of the ovens isn't working and I can't figure out what is wrong."

"I'll be there shortly."

Hanging up, he went over to Courtney. "I have to run to the warehouse. Do you want to come along?"

"No, I don't think so. I'm just going to hang out for a bit."

"Okay." Leaning over, he kissed her and left.

After discovering the oven was dead, Brian got into his

car and reached over to the glove box to retrieve his phone book of vendors. Digging through the papers, he came across the little box with the ring in it he had purchased last month. He had bought it on a whim but tucked it away quickly and hid it out of sight. After he made his call to order a new oven, he sat in his car with the little box in his hand.

He opened it.

The ring was a white gold band with a bridge over water design and a princess-cut diamond at the center. He smiled as he thought over the last nine months of dating Courtney. She was everything he wanted in a woman and in a helpmate.

Closing the box, he set it in the passenger seat and drove out to the Spokane Valley cemetery where his father was buried. The sun was beginning to set as he climbed the grassy hill to where his father was buried facing the railroad tracks. He sat down next to the headstone and peered at the setting sun in the distance.

"Dad, I think she's the one." Pulling the ring box out from his jacket pocket, he popped it open and stared at the ring. "I'm so scared of the unknown. Scared of what could happen. I don't want to have a second divorce. I already lost one wife I thought I'd spend my life with."

A train came roaring down the railroad tracks in the distant sunset. He recalled his father's time working on the railroad and how he'd run and jump onto the moving trains. He had a thought come to his mind in that very moment. *You can't catch the train if you don't jump.*

Bowing his head, he prayed. "God, I'm not sure what to do, but what I am sure of is You. You've been with me and You have carried me all throughout my life. You've guided me, led me, and taught me Your way and Your desires for my life."

Moving to a knee a short while later, Brian looked at his

father's name engraved into the stone. Tracing the letters of his name with his fingers, he longed to have five more minutes with the man who had raised him. Peering over at his dad's fourth wife's gravestone beside him, he shook his head and dipped his chin. "I miss you, Dad, but I don't want to repeat your history."

TAKING ONE MORE BITE OF her fried rice from the Chinese takeout box, she set the container down on the coffee table and snuggled up on the couch under her red and black plaid blanket. Brian had left hours ago and she hadn't heard from him since. She figured he'd ended up going home after the warehouse. She understood if he had gone home. With how emotional she had been today, she wouldn't have wanted to spend a lot of time around her, either.

A knock sounded on the door of her apartment and she paused her movie. Her heart ticked up and her lips curled into a smile as she pushed the blanket off and went to answer the door.

It was Brian.

"Hey. I brought takeout." He held up a plastic bag of Chinese food.

She laughed and pointed to the coffee table and her takeout boxes.

"Great minds think alike." Walking inside, he set the food on the counter. "Sorry it took so long. I went and saw my dad. It was the anniversary of his death yesterday."

"Oh, wow. I didn't know that."

"Yep. Ten years." His eyes went to the TV. "What are you watching?"

"Just a sappy chick flick."

He smiled and walked over with her to the couch. "It's a good thing I love you."

Her heart warmed at his playfulness. Sitting down together, they started watching the movie together while he ate. After he finished eating, she snuggled up against his chest with her blanket tucked around her. Unable to control the heaviness in her eyes as the night wore on, she fell asleep in his arms.

Waking the next morning, still on the couch, she looked around for Brian, but he wasn't there.

Standing up, she walked over to the coffee pot and found it had been freshly brewed. Smiling, she grabbed for a cup out of the cupboard, but she noticed something.

A ring on her finger.

Confusion filled her thoughts as she brought the hand slowly down from the cupboard. *Wait.*

The front door of the apartment opened just then, startling her. She spun around quickly to face the door.

It was Brian, and he had a bag of fresh bagels from the bakery down the road.

"Dang. You're up? I was going to surprise you." He shut the door and came over to her in the kitchen.

Raising her eyebrows as her smile grew, she showed her left hand to him. "I think you still did surprise me."

He came closer to her as he set the bagels down on the counter. "So? Will you?"

Waves of excitement and joy washed over her from head to toe. "Yes! I will marry you!"

Hoisting her up into his arms, he spun her around and set her back down gently. He kissed her deeply and peered into her eyes.

"I'm so happy you said yes."

"I'm so happy you asked! After the emotional day I had

yesterday and then your leaving, I thought you weren't coming back."

"Aw. Of course I was coming back. I want to be here for you. Not just here and there, but every day for the rest of our lives." They kissed again and then went and sat on the couch, forgetting the bagels entirely. "You've been a blessing in my life, Courtney, and I couldn't imagine not seeing you every day."

Her smile grew as the warmth of love filled her heart. "You are an amazing man of God, and I couldn't ask for a better husband."

Saying the word *husband* jogged her memory of the letter Drew had written for when he had passed. Hesitation filled her for a moment as she thought about whether to show him the letter.

Brian touched her hand. "What is it?"

"I want to show you something. It might be weird for you, but it's important to me."

"Anything. If it's important to you, I want to see it no matter how weird it is."

She smiled. "I'll be right back."

Walking down the hallway to her bedroom, she went in and over to the dresser. Grabbing the envelope, she returned to the living room. Sitting down on the couch, she set the letter in her lap and placed both hands on top of it. "You already know about Drew."

"Yes."

"*Well,* he wrote a letter to me that I later found in his desk. It was in the event that he were to die when we were younger."

Raising his eyebrows, Brian nodded slowly. "Okay."

"He wanted me to remarry if I was young, and . . ." Shaking her head as she became lost for words, she just handed it to him. "This is what he wrote."

Taking the envelope, he opened it and pulled out the letter. He read it with tears in his eyes and peered up at Courtney. "What a beautiful gift."

Smiling, Courtney nodded and received the letter and envelope back into her hands. "You meet every one of his requirements, Brian. He wrote a letter about *you*."

"Wow. I bet that letter helped you a lot."

She nodded. "It did."

"Thank you for sharing that with me."

"You're welcome." The smell of the freshly baked bagels caught Courtney's attention. "Let's dig into those bagels!"

CHAPTER 14

*O*n Thanksgiving, two weeks before the wedding, Brian and Courtney were celebrating the holidays with Lucy, Rhonda, Taylor, and the boys at Brian's house. The turkey was ready and it was time to get everyone to the table. Shutting off the football game on the television, Brian got off the couch and went down the hallway to where Lucy and the boys were playing board games.

"It's time for dinner, kids."

The boys jumped up and sprinted for the door. Lucy was a little slower. Brian came in close and pulled her in for a side hug. "I'm glad your mother let you be here this year, Princess."

"It's nice. I heard Mom and Conrad talking the other day, and they said they'd come to the wedding if they were invited. Are you going to invite them, Dad?"

Smiling, he nodded. "Sure! The more the merrier. Right?"

Lucy smiled and nodded, side hugging her dad a little tighter as they exited the room. It did his heart a great deal of joy to hear that the two of them wouldn't just go to the wedding but *wanted* to come to it. Lifting a prayer of thanks toward Heaven, he knew it was the work of God on their hearts and an answer to prayer.

Arriving at the dining room and the head of the table, Brian stepped out of the way of Courtney as she walked in with the turkey on a platter. Setting it down on the table, she turned toward him. He slid his hand along her back and pulled her in for a kiss.

"The bird looks marvelous, dear."

"You can thank my mother for that." Glancing over at Rhonda, she smiled at her mom.

Brian was reminded of Lucy's mention of Melissa and Conrad and he explained to his bride-to-be what he had learned.

Courtney nodded. "That'd be awesome if they came to the wedding!"

"It wouldn't be weird since it's my ex-wife?"

She shrugged. "Who cares if it's weird?"

He smiled. "Fantastic."

Turning to everyone, he raised his voice. "Let's all lock hands and pray over the food."

Everyone stood around the table holding hands as Brian led the Thanksgiving prayer. "As another year in our lives passes, Lord, let us remember to be thankful toward You. Not just today, but every day and for every day we have each other. We never know when it's the last Thanksgiving we'll have. We never know when it's the last time we will see a loved one. You are so gracious, so kind, so loving to us, God. Now as we sit down and enjoy this wonderful food, let us radiate Your love in our conversations, Your love in our lives. We pray all these things in Your precious and Holy name, Jesus, Amen."

After the meal a short while later and when everyone was heading toward that nappy feeling, the doorbell chimes rang through the house.

"That's probably Mom." Lucy stood from the table and pushed in her chair.

"I'll walk you." Brian rose from his seat. Kissing Courtney on the cheek, he accompanied his daughter to the door. Lucy ran out to the car and got in while Melissa tarried for a moment.

"How was your Thanksgiving?"

Brian smiled. "Great. I really appreciate your letting her be here this year. It was a treat having her. How was yours?"

"It was good, and you're welcome. I think we should revisit the schedule with her. Maybe let her come over more weekends than just once a month. She was saying the other day that she'd like that."

Raising an eyebrow, he nodded in agreement. "I like that idea too. Hey. Do you and Conrad want to come to the wedding? Courtney and I would love to have you."

"Yeah, we would!" Melissa smiled as she looked back at the car. "Lucy told you about Conrad's and my conversation, I take it."

Brian laughed. "Yes, she did."

Melissa turned to Brian as she nodded. "I see. I feel like I should tell you that I started seeing a counselor at a church recently. Conrad and I started going to church too. I've realized a lot of what's been wrong with me had nothing to do with you but was about my relationship with God."

"Wow. That's great to hear you're back in church, Melissa."

"It is great, but it's also hard to realize how wrong I was for what I did. I'm so sorry."

Holding up his hand, Brian shook his head. "You've already been forgiven."

Melissa teared up and nodded, then shifted her footing toward the car. "That means a lot. Thank you. I'd better get going. Have a good rest of your Thanksgiving."

"Okay. Take care and have a good night."

Shutting the door, he turned around and peered up at the ceiling. *You are so amazing, God! When I just step out of the way and give things time, You resolve them in Your timing and I am able to see You work! Thank You.*

Bringing his gaze down, he walked back into the dining room. He saw Courtney and Taylor laughing hysterically about something, but he didn't know what. Peering over at Rhonda, he saw her looking at a book Todd was showing her. He smiled. These people coming together, and all of this love under one roof, was only possible and plausible by the love of God working in all of their lives. A tug on the corner of his sweatshirt pulled his attention downward. It was Blaze.

Lowering himself to eye level with the two-year-old, he raised an eyebrow. "Yeah, Blaze?"

"Can you make a ramp for me?" Holding out his hand, he had a little shiny silver toy car in his hand.

"Sure." He rubbed his head. "Let's go make one."

STANDING IN FRONT OF A mirror in the dressing room at the church, Courtney smiled as she twirled her wedding dress and train. She never dreamed she'd be in another one of these, not after Drew. Her mother and Taylor were there with her, helping make sure everything was perfect for her big day.

Turning to her mother, she noticed tears.

"What's wrong, Mom?"

Shaking her head, she came closer and touched her hand gently. "When you lost Drew, I never thought you'd be okay again. It brings my heart so much joy to see you happy."

Taylor came over and handed Courtney a glass of sparkling cider as she smiled. "He's perfect for you, Sis! You two are going to have tons of babies and be happy forever! Like you always wanted!"

Her heart warmed and eased the pre-ceremony jitters. "Thank you. Both of you."

The door of the dressing room door opened and Lucy walked in.

Courtney smiled. Her and Lucy's relationship had grown in leaps and bounds over the last few months, and while she'd never replace Melissa, nor did she want to, she knew they had a special connection.

"Good morning, Lucy. Your dress is over in the closet."

Lucy came over to her and handed her a small white box.

"*Oh?* What's this?" Taking the box, she opened it and pulled out tissue paper.

As she unfolded it, Lucy spoke. "It's something I picked out for you and my dad."

The gift was an 'Our First Christmas' ornament. Stepping down from the platform, Courtney hugged Lucy. "Thank you. That's so sweet of you!"

"You make my dad happy and he loves you . . . and so do I."

"Aw!" Wiping tears from her cheeks, Courtney tilted her head and smiled. "I love you too."

After Lucy took her dress and shut the door to the bathroom, Taylor turned toward Courtney. "She's so mature for twelve."

"She really is, and she's acting older a little more each day."

Going back to the mirror, Courtney asked how much longer.

Her sister joined her gaze into the mirror. "Five minutes. Are you two going to try for a baby right away?"

"Taylor!" Rhonda scolded her.

Courtney giggled. "We're not going to fight against it!"

———

AFTER THE FIRST DANCE WITH his bride, Brian went searching for the second-most important lady in his life. Finding her sitting at the children's table, he extended a hand to Lucy as he bowed.

"May I have this dance, Princess?"

She lit up and placed her hand in his hand. Leading his daughter to the dance floor as *Butterfly Kisses* began to play by his request to the DJ, they started to dance.

"Cool wedding, Dad."

Smiling, he raised an eyebrow and glanced at her. "Yeah? You want something like this for when you get married to your future pastor husband?"

They both laughed.

Lucy rested her head against his chest as they swayed to the music. Brian's heart was heavy knowing his little girl was growing up before his eyes. Memories flashed through his mind of slow dancing with her in his arms as a toddler. Slow dancing with her at their small house with wood paneling on the walls. Now he was dancing with her without having to hold her in his arms. Holding Lucy close, he prayed over her and her future.

After their dance, Brian caught up with Courtney and went around to tables talking to various guests who had come to celebrate. The majority of people who attended were members of their church. There were also a handful of employees from the warehouse and a few friends.

Finding their way to Melissa and Conrad's table, they both sat down with them.

"Awesome wedding, man." Conrad took a drink of his water. "I thought dancing wasn't okay in church."

Brian shrugged. "Some churches are stiffer about it, but this one isn't."

Melissa directed her gaze toward Courtney. "You look lovely. I'm so happy you're Lucy's stepmother. I couldn't ask for a better woman to be a part of her life other than me."

"Aw. That means so much to me!" Courtney stood up and they both hugged.

"Can we skip the hug part?" Brian remarked jokingly.

Conrad nodded with raised eyebrows. "We can do a fist bump."

They fist bumped and then proceeded to laugh. Lifting a heart of thanks to God in that moment, Brian felt right then that he was experiencing the Scriptural truth that *all things are possible with God*. Not in a millennium would he have pictured himself casually chatting with Conrad and Melissa as if they were friends. It was an act of God that it was possible.

As the night was winding down and Brian was sitting at a table with Courtney, he looked over to the dance floor and saw Lucy with Todd and Blaze. He smiled as he saw all three of them throw their arms back and forth while they shook their bodies to the tune of the music playing.

Courtney leaned over into Brian's ear. "That's cute."

Glancing at her, he nodded. "It is adorable." Fully turning toward her, he took her hands in his. "I don't want to wait to have kids."

She blushed. "Neither do I."

CHAPTER 15

Waking in the wee hours of the morning one December night, the year following their wedding, Courtney rolled over in bed to see Brian wasn't there. Rubbing her eyes, she sat up and looked over at the clock on the nightstand. It was two o'clock in the morning. Pushing off the covers, she left their bedroom and traveled down the hallway. Going into her old office, she pushed open the door and peeked in.

Brian was sitting in the rocking chair by the window, feeding their two-week-old baby boy a bottle. Her heart melted knowing he had let her sleep instead of waking her.

Proceeding into the room and over to him, she peered down at the newborn baby's face, barely visible in the low light.

Softly, she spoke. "He's so sweet and precious."

"I know." Carefully standing up from the rocking chair, Brian placed the child back into the crib.

They walked out of the room together and Brian quietly shut the door behind him.

"I think I have a name I like." Courtney hadn't been able

to settle on a name since he was born, so they were waiting to officially name the child.

"Okay. What are you thinking?"

"Isaac."

"It's perfect." He leaned in and kissed her. Taking her by the hand, he led her back to their bedroom and they both fell back into slumber quickly.

That evening was Courtney's Thursday night Bible study with the ladies. Leaving baby Isaac with Brian at home, she headed over to her sister's house to pick her up. She had started joining her last month. Getting to the door of the apartment, she knocked and then walked inside.

"Where are Todd and Blaze?"

Taylor grabbed her purse from the counter. "At the movies with Grandma."

"Nice. We picked a name—Isaac."

Smiling, Taylor nodded. "I like that name. Hey. I wanted you to have this."

Courtney watched as she walked over to a bookcase in the living room and grabbed the scrapbook Courtney had given to her.

"What? I gave that to you."

"I know." Handing it to Courtney, she smiled. "But during this time, the boys were yours. They weren't mine at all. I know you cherished the time you had with them, and I think keeping this is a great way for you to do that. I loved seeing the evidence of the love and fun times they had with you while I was gone, but now it's just a painful reminder of a bad time in my life."

Taking the scrapbook from her sister, Courtney pulled it in close to her chest and hugged it close. "Thank you."

"I don't regret anything that happened, and I'm thankful for all that you did for me and the boys, Courtney. I'll forever remember it. You gave everything while expecting nothing in return."

"That's not entirely true."

"What do you mean?"

"I got to love on those boys for eleven months. I got to experience motherhood without being a biological mother. And you know what else? It led me to Brian. We both know I wouldn't have actively dated or sought out a man, but the circumstances led me right to his arms. So really, thank *you*, Taylor."

Hugging, they both lightly wept and then went to the ladies' Bible study.

WITH ISAAC SLEEPING ON HIS chest and himself sprawled out on the couch, listening to the football game quietly on the television, Brian stared at the ceiling and thought about how wonderful God was to him. Delicately lifting Isaac from his chest, he went down to the nursery and tucked him into his crib. Before leaving, he rested the palm of his hand on Isaac's tummy and prayed over him.

"Lord, protect him. Strengthen him. Teach his spirit Your wonderful ways. Help me to be the father You are to me. Help me to raise him in Your truth, wisdom, and power. Amen."

Walking out of the nursery, he closed the door behind him and returned to the living room. Grabbing the television remote, he shut the TV off and walked over to the windows overlooking the back yard.

It was snowing, and the flakes caught light from the light pole out in the yard. Watching as the snow delicately fell to the ground, he thought about each flake's unique design and creation. He was reminded of Courtney's comment on the matter years ago when they were dating.

His lips curled into a smile. Brian knew God's design and desires for his life were far grander and far more beautiful than he could ever dream. God's design had led him to Courtney, led him to getting married again, and led him to having a son.

Courtney soon arrived home, breaking his thoughts and concentration away from the falling snow outside the window.

Meeting her in the kitchen as she flipped on the light, he asked how the evening went.

"Good." She set the scrapbook down on the kitchen island.

"I thought you gave that to your sister."

She smiled, looking at it, and then came around the island to Brian. Wrapping her arms around his neck, she leaned up and kissed him.

"I did, but she gave it back to me. You know, I think I realized the meaning of life tonight."

"Wow. Must've been some Bible study, huh?" They both lightly laughed. Then he asked, "What do you mean?"

"Life is not about the love we get from other people but the love we already have from God. It's about a relationship with God. Then the true meaning in life comes to us as we extend that love He gives us to other people. In this way, we learn to love in His way."

"I couldn't agree more." Leaning in, he kissed her.

The End.
Be sure to check out book 3, "Trusting Him To Lead"
View On Amazon

A REASON TO LIVE PREVIEW

Chapter 1

POUNDING COMING FROM THE FRONT door of his house on the South Hill woke Jonathan Dunken from sleep at three o'clock in the morning. Then the doorbell chimed, pulling him further away from his slumber and fully awake. He had only been asleep for an hour, as he had been up late the night before sketching building concepts for a client. He was the co-founder and sole architect of his and his brother Tyler's company, *Willow Design*. A company the two of them started just a few years ago, after Marie passed and Jonathan needed more work to throw himself into.

Pushing his eyelids open, he sat up in his bed, smoothing a hand over his face. *Who on earth is that?* He wondered. The doorbell chimed again, and he begrudgingly emerged from his bed and left his bedroom.

He traveled out from his room, through the long hallway, and down the glass stairs. As he entered the foyer, more pounding on the door sounded, edging his already growing irritation. He was ready to rip into whoever was on the other side of that door. But when he finally opened it, his heart plunged and the wind fanning his anger fell quiet. It was his sister-in-law, Shawna Gillshock, a woman he hadn't seen since the funeral four years ago.

Shawna looked just like he remembered her—a mess, her brunette hair disheveled, eyeliner mingled with rainwater ran down each of her cheeks. She was wearing a stained pair of ragged sweats three times too big and a ragged oversized hooded sweatshirt. He immediately noticed the sight of fresh blood on a cut near her left eyebrow.

"I need your help, Jonathan. I didn't know where else to go." Her voice was strained, filled with desperation. She jerked her head toward the car in the driveway. Sheets of rain and wind whipped back and forth in the night's air, dancing across the headlights of the car. "My dad wouldn't let me come to his house. I need a place for me and my daughter, Rose, to stay tonight. My boyfriend beat me again, and I'm leaving him for good this time. You're the only person I know that he doesn't know. Please?"

Jonathan was moved with compassion, though a part of him wanted to say 'no' to her. Deep down, somewhere beneath the pain and grief that followed losing his wife, he heard a whisper and felt a nudge. *Let her stay.*

"Okay. You can stay." He helped her inside with her luggage and daughter. The luggage she had brought didn't consist of much. A backpack and one suitcase. Once the two of them had everything inside the house in the foyer, he led the way to the guest room on the main floor of the two-story house. The room was tucked away at the end of the hallway. Opening the door, he flipped on the light switch. Two lamps, one on each nightstand on either side of the bed, turned on. Each of the nightstands, along with the dresser and crown molding, was stark white. The walls were a warm brown, not dark, but not light either. On the far side of the bedroom, near the dresser, was another doorway leading into an en-suite bathroom.

"Thank you so much for this." Her words were filled with genuine gratitude as she set her backpack on the bed. She turned and glanced at the TV on top of the dresser.

"How long do you think you'll be here, Shawna?" Jonathan was gently reminding her it wasn't a long-term solution but more of a friendly gesture in a time of need.

"Just a few days. I'm going to call my dad again tomorrow and see if I can convince him to let us stay there with him and Betty until I can figure something out."

The mention of her parents jogged painful memories that Jonathan had tried to forget. His parents had died his senior year of high school, so he only really had Marie's parents in his life. "Okay, and if he doesn't budge?"

Shawna turned to face him. "I'll figure something out. Don't worry about me, just thanks again for tonight."

Her daughter became fussy a moment later, a whimper escaping. "What's wrong, Rose?"

She touched her tummy. "I'm hungry."

"How old is she?"

Smiling, Shawna turned to him. "She's two. Talking away already. Do you have anything she can eat?"

Scrambling through the fridge in his mind, he shrugged. "Does she like tuna?"

"Um, not really. Do you have hot dogs, macaroni, or something more kid-friendly like that?"

"No, but there are eggs in the fridge. Sorry. I wasn't really prepared for you." He tipped a smile, trying to loosen the awkwardness and embrace the disturbance of the entire situation.

She laughed lightly. "It's totally fine. Eggs work great. She loves scrambled eggs. Thank you again, Jonathan. It means the world that you took us in tonight."

"Don't mention it. Do you need help cooking, or can you manage it?"

"It's pretty basic. I think I got it handled. You look like you need some sleep, so go ahead."

"I do need sleep. Going back to bed now. 'Night."

Leaving Shawna and Rose in the guest room, he shut the door quietly and thought of his late wife, Marie, as he made his way back to his bedroom upstairs. Shawna was his only sister-in-law, and she had made frequent appearances in his and Marie's life, but that had been years ago. Even back in the day, Shawna was always in need. Her life reminded him of a slow-moving train wreck in progress. Though her life was a wreck, Marie was always ready and willing to love on her and care for her when she was in need of her big sister. That was Marie's nature with not only family, but anyone who was in need.

Did you enjoy this free sample? Find it on Amazon

ONE THURSDAY MORNING PREVIEW

Prologue

To love and be loved—it was all I ever wanted. Nobody could ever convince me John was a bad man. He made me feel loved when I did not know what love was. I was his and he was mine. It was perfect . . . or at least, I thought it was.

I cannot pinpoint why everything changed in our lives, but it did—and for the worst. My protector, my savior, and my whole world came crashing down like a heavy spring downpour. The first time he struck me, I remember thinking it was just an accident. He had been drinking earlier in the day with his friends and came stumbling home late that night. The lights were low throughout the house because I had already gone to bed. I remember hearing the car pull up outside in the driveway. Leaping to my feet, I came rushing downstairs and through the kitchen to greet him. He swung, which I thought at the time was because I startled him, and the back side of his hand caught my cheek.

I should have known it wasn't an accident.

The second time was no accident at all, and I knew it. After a heavy night of drinking the night his father died, he came to the study where I was reading. Like a hunter looking for his prey, he came up behind me to the couch. Grabbing the back of my head and digging his fingers into my hair, he kinked my neck over the couch and asked me why I hadn't been faithful to him. I had no idea what he was talking about, so out of sheer fear, I began to cry. John took that as a sign of guilt and backhanded me across the face. It was hard enough to leave a bruise the following day. I stayed with him anyway. I'd put a little extra makeup on around my eyes or anywhere else when marks were left. I didn't stay because I was stupid, but because I loved him. I kept telling myself that our love could get us through this. The night of his father's death, I blamed his outburst on the loss of his father. It was too much for him to handle, and he was just letting out steam. I swore to love him through the good times and the bad. This was just one of the bad times.

Each time he'd hit me, I'd come up with a reason or excuse for the behavior. There was always a reason, at least in my mind, as to why John hit me. Then one time, after a really bad injury, I sought help from my mother before she passed away. The closest thing to a saint on earth, she dealt with my father's abuse for decades before he died. She was a devout Christian, but a warped idea of love plagued my mother her entire life. She told me, 'What therefore God hath joined together, let not man put asunder.' That one piece of advice she gave me months before passing made me suffer through a marriage with John for another five trying years.

Each day with John as a husband was a day full of prayer. I would pray for him not to drink, and sometimes, he didn't —those were the days I felt God had listened to my pleas. On the days he came home drunk and swinging, I felt alone, like God had left me to die by my husband's hands. Fear was a cornerstone of our relationship, in my eyes, and I hated it. As the years piled onto one another, I began to deal with two entirely different people when it came to John. There was the John who would give me everything I need in life and bring flowers home on the days he was sober, and then there was John, the drunk, who would bring insults and injury instead of flowers.

I knew something needed to desperately change in my life, but I didn't have the courage. Then one day, it all changed when two little pink lines told me to run and never look back.

Chapter 1

Fingers glided against the skin of my arm as I lay on my side looking into John's big, gorgeous brown eyes. It was morning, so I knew he was sober, and for a moment, I thought maybe, just maybe I could tell him about the baby growing inside me. Flashes of a shared excitement between us blinked through my mind. He'd love having a baby around the house. *He really would.* Behind those eyes, I saw the man I fell in love with years ago down in Town Square in New York City. Those eyes were the same ones that brought me into a world of love and security I had never known before. Moments like that made it hard to hate him. Peering over at his hand that was tracing the side of my body, I saw the cut on his knuckles from where he had smashed the coffee table a few nights ago. My heart retracted the notion of telling him about the baby. I knew John would be dangerous for a child.

Chills shivered up my spine as his fingers traced from my arm to the curve of my back. *Could I be strong enough to live without him?* I wondered as the fears sank back down into me. Even if he was a bit mean, he had a way of charming me like no other man I had ever met in my life. He knew how to touch gently, look deeply and make love passionately. It was only when he drank that his demons came out.

"Want me to make you some breakfast?" I asked, slipping out of his touch and from the bed to my feet. His touches were enjoyable, but I wanted to get used to not having them. My mind often jumped back and forth between leaving, not leaving, and something vaguely in between. It was hard.

John smiled up at me from the bed with what made me feel like love in his eyes. I suddenly began to feel bad about the plan to leave, but I knew he couldn't be trusted with a child. *Keep it together.*

"Sure, babe. That'd be great." He brought his muscular arms from out of the covers and put them behind his head. My eyes traced his biceps and face. Wavy brown hair and a jawline that was defined made him breathtakingly gorgeous. Flashes of last night's passion bombarded my mind. He didn't drink, and that meant one thing—we made love. It started in the main living room just off the foyer. I was enjoying my evening cup of tea while the fireplace was lit when suddenly, John came home early. I was worried at first, but when he leaned over the couch and pulled back my blonde hair, he planted a tender kiss on my neck. I knew right in that moment that it was going to be a good night. Hoisting me up from the couch with those arms and pressing me against the wall near the fireplace, John's passion fell from his lips and onto the skin of my neck as I wrapped my arms around him.

The heat between John and me was undeniable, and it

made the thoughts of leaving him that much harder. It was during those moments of pure passion that I could still see the bits of the John I once knew—the part of John that didn't scare me and had the ability to make me feel safe, and the part of him that I never wanted to lose.

"All right," I replied with a smile as I broke away from my thoughts. Leaving down the hallway, I pushed last night out of my mind and focused on the tasks ahead.

Retrieving the carton of eggs from the fridge in the kitchen, I shut the door and was startled when John was standing on the other side. Jumping, I let out a squeak. "John!"

He tilted his head and slipped closer to me. With nothing on but his boxer briefs, he backed me against the counter and let his hand slide the corner of my shirt up my side. He leaned closer to me. I felt the warmth of his breath on my skin as my back arched against the counter top. He licked his lips instinctively to moisten them and then gently let them find their way to my neck. "Serenah . . ." he said in a smooth, seductive voice.

"Let me make you breakfast," I said as I set the carton down on the counter behind me and turned my neck into him to stop the kissing.

His eyebrows rose as he pulled away from my body and released. His eyes met mine. There it was—the change. "*Fine.*"

"What?" I replied as I turned and pulled down a frying pan that hung above the island counter.

"Nothing. Nothing. I have to go shower." He left down the hallway without a word, but I could sense tension in his tone.

Waiting for the shower to turn on after he walked into the bathroom and slammed the door, I began to cook his eggs. When a few minutes had passed and I hadn't heard the water start running, I lifted my eyes and looked down the hallway.

There he was.

John stood at the end of hallway, watching me. Standing in the shifting shadows of the long hallway, he was more than creepy. He often did that type of thing, but it came later in the marriage, not early on and only at home. I never knew how long he was standing there before I caught him, but he'd always break away after being seen. He had a sick obsession of studying me like I was some sort of weird science project of his.

I didn't like it all, but it was part of who he had become. *Not much longer,* I reminded myself.

I smiled down the hallway at him, and he returned to the bathroom to finally take his shower. As I heard the water come on, I finished the eggs and set the frying pan off the burner. Dumping the eggs onto a plate, I set the pan in the sink and headed to the piano in the main living room. Pulling the bench out from under the piano, I got down on my hands and knees and lifted the flap of carpet that was squared off. Removing the plank of wood that concealed my secret area, I retrieved the metal box and opened it.

Freedom.

Ever since he hit me that second time, a part of me knew we'd never have the forever marriage I pictured, so in case I was right, I began saving money here and there. I had been able to save just over ten thousand dollars. A fibbed high-priced manicure here, a few non-existent shopping trips with friends there. It added up, and John had not the foggiest clue, since he was too much of an egomaniac to pay attention to anything that didn't directly affect him. Sure, it was his money, but money wasn't really 'a thing' to us. We were beyond that. My eyes looked at the money in the stash and then over at the bus ticket to Seattle dated for four days from now. I could hardly believe it. I was really going to finally leave him after all this time. Amongst the cash and bus ticket, there was a cheap pay-as-you go cellphone and a fake ID. I had to check that box at least once a day ever since I found out about my pregnancy to make sure he hadn't found it. I was scared to leave, but whenever I felt that way, I rubbed my pregnant thirteen-week belly, and I knew I had to do what was best for *us*. Putting the box back into the floor, I was straightening out the carpet when suddenly, John's breathing settled into my ears behind me.

"What are you doing?" he asked, towel draped around his waist behind me. *I should have just waited until he left for work . . . What were you thinking, Serenah?* My thoughts scolded me.

Slamming my head into the bottom of the piano, I grabbed my head and backed out as I let out a groan. "There was a crumb on the carpet."

"What? Underneath the piano?" he asked.

Anxiety rose within me like a storm at sea. Using the bench for leverage, I placed a hand on it and began to get up. When I didn't respond to his question quick enough, he shoved my arm that was propped on the piano bench, causing me to smash my eye into the corner of the bench. Pain radiated through my skull as I cupped my eye and began to cry.

"Oh, please. That barely hurt you."

I didn't respond. Falling the rest of the way to the floor, I cupped my eye and hoped he'd just leave. Letting out a heavy sigh, he got down, still in his towel, and put his hand on my shoulder. "I'm sorry, honey."

Jerking my shoulder away from him, I replied, "Go away!"

He stood up and left.

John hurt me sober? Rising to my feet, I headed into the half-bathroom across the living room and looked into the mirror. My eye was blood red—he had popped a blood vessel. Tears welled in my eyes as my eyebrows furrowed in disgust.

Four days wasn't soon enough to leave—I was leaving today.

Did you enjoy this free sample? Find it on Amazon

FREE GIFT

Cole has fought hundreds of fires in his lifetime, but he had never tasted fear until he came to fighting a fire in his own home. *Amongst The Flames* is a Christian firefighter fiction that tackles real-life situations and problems that exist in Christian marriages today. It brings with it passion, love and spiritual depth that will leave you feeling inspired. This Inspirational Christian romance novel is one book that you'll want to read over and over again.

To Claim Visit:
offer.tkchapin.com

ALSO BY T.K. CHAPIN

A Reason To Love Series

A Reason To Live (Book 1)

A Reason To Believe (Book 2)

A Reason To Forgive (Book 3)

A Reason To Trust (Book 4)

Journey Of Love Series

Journey Of Grace (Book 1)

Journey Of Hope (Book 2)

Journey Of Faith (Book 3)

Protected By Love Series

Love's Return (Book 1)

Love's Promise (Book 2)

Love's Protection (Book 3)

Diamond Lake Series

One Thursday Morning (Book 1)

One Friday Afternoon (Book 2)

One Saturday Evening (Book 3)

One Sunday Drive (Book 4)

One Monday Prayer (Book 5)

One Tuesday Lunch (Book 6)

One Wednesday Dinner (Book 7)

Embers & Ashes Series

Amongst the Flames (Book 1)

Out of the Ashes (Book 2)

Up in Smoke (Book 3)

After the Fire (Book 4)

Love's Enduring Promise Series

The Perfect Cast (Book 1)

Finding Love (Book 2)

Claire's Hope (Book 3)

Dylan's Faith (Book 4)

Stand Alones

Love Interrupted

Love Again

A Chance at Love

The Broken Road

If Only

Because Of You

The Lies We Believe

In His Love

When It Rains

Gracefully Broken

Please join T.K. Chapin's Mailing List to be notified
of upcoming releases and promotions.

Join the List

ACKNOWLEDGMENTS

First and foremost, I want to thank God. God's salvation through the death, burial and resurrection of Jesus Christ gives us all the ability to have a personal relationship with the Creator of the Universe.

I also want to thank my wife. She's my muse and my inspiration. A wonderful wife, an amazing mother and the best person I have ever met. She's great and has always stood by me with every decision I have made along life's way.

I'd like to thank my editors and early readers for helping me along the way. I also want to thank all of my friends and extended family for the support. It's a true blessing to have every person I know in my life.

ABOUT THE AUTHOR

 **T.K. CHAPIN** writes Christian Romance books designed to inspire and tug on your heart strings. He believes that telling stories of faith, love and family help build the faith of Christians and help non-believers see how God can work in the life of believers. He gives all credit for his writing and storytelling ability to God. The majority of the novels take place in and around Spokane, Washington, his hometown. Chapin makes his home in Idaho and has the pleasure of raising his daughter and two sons with his beautiful wife Crystal.

Learn more by visiting
www.tkchapin.com

facebook.com/officialtkchapin

twitter.com/tkchapin

instagram.com/tkchapin